05

Powerful Classroom Stories from Accomplished Teachers

D1056723

To the millions of children who fill our classrooms
and to the amazing teachers who teach them.
These are their stories.

Adrienne Mack-Kirschner
Foreword by Cathy Owens

Powerful Classroom Stories from Accomplished Teachers

OAKTON COMMUNITY COLLEGE
DES PLAINES CAMPUS
1600 EAST GOLF ROAD
DES PLAINES, IL 60016

CORWIN PRESS
A Sage Publications Company
Thousand Oaks, California

For information:

Corwin Press
A Sage Publications Company
2455 Teller Road
Thousand Oaks, California 91320
www.corwinpress.com

Sage Publications Ltd.
6 Bonhill Street
London EC2A 4PU
United Kingdom

Sage Publications India Pvt. Ltd.
B-42, Panchsheel Enclave
Post Box 4109
New Delhi 110 017 India

Printed in the United States of America

Library of Congress Cataloging-in-Publication Data

Mack-Kirschner, Adrienne, 1944-
Powerful classroom stories from accomplished teachers / Adrienne Mack-Kirschner.
        p. cm.
Includes bibliographical references and index.
ISBN 0-7619-3911-3 (Cloth) — ISBN 0-7619-3912-1 (Paper)
    1. Effective teaching—United States—Case studies. 2. Teachers—United States—Case studies. I. Title.
LB1025.3.M334 2004
371.102—dc21

                                                           2003012432

03   04   05   06   10   9   8   7   6   5   4   3   2   1

Acquisitions Editor:	Faye Zucker
Editorial Assistant:	Stacy Wagner
Production Editor:	Melanie Birdsall
Copy Editor:	Toni Williams
Typesetter:	C&M Digitals (P) Ltd.
Proofreader:	Kristin Bergstad
Indexer:	Michael Ferreira
Cover Designer:	Michael Dubowe
Graphic Designer:	Lisa Miller

Contents

Foreword

Never before has the need been so great for classroom teachers to assume leadership roles that position them as problem solvers and change agents in their local schools. Teachers know students best, and the stories in this book provide compelling evidence of the impact accomplished teachers can and do have on students and their learning. *Powerful Classroom Stories from Accomplished Teachers* shows us how we, as teacher leaders in collaboration with other accomplished teachers, can ensure that schooling is improved. Teaching is our profession and it is our responsibility to strengthen it.

Teacher leaders know what the challenging questions are: How do we accommodate the needs of at-risk students while simultaneously responding to the needs of advanced learners? How do we reallocate human and fiscal resources to achieve balance in schooling across districts and states? How do we use test results and achievement data to better assess student learning? How do we identify highly qualified teaching in an effort to better prepare those who enter teaching through alternative routes so that all children have access to quality instruction?

But many accomplished teachers don't think about the answers to these questions. Many of us do not engage in the professional dialogue that leads to solutions to the challenges we face. Typically, our conversations begin and end with the problems in schools. We go into our classrooms, close our doors, and do what we have always done. Nor has teacher leadership been on the reform agenda. Education officials have consistently thought they might reform schools by bringing in a new program, a new model, and a new initiative from the outside. But history teaches us that what really transforms schools into learning environments for both students and faculty is a reform movement that starts from within the school and is driven by those who have the greatest stake in its success or failure. The power of improving education one school at a time is realized when a mixed team within the school—a true professional learning community—comes to the table to engage in meaningful dialogue about where they are, where they want to be, and what they themselves can do to get there. This is the only way to prevent any child from being left behind.

Too much of what goes on in schools is automatic. Leaders in education policy continue to get the same results because they continue to employ the same traditional methodologies. But this is not true of National Board Certified Teachers (NBCTs). As members of a larger learning community, NBCTs engage in professional collaborations that contribute to the overall effectiveness of schools. They assume leadership roles, in addition to the direct instruction of students, that will help effect positive change in how teachers teach, how students learn, and how schools operate.

Achieving National Board Certification taught me that going into my classroom and closing the door is never going to reform education. Sharing my practice with other colleagues, educating parents and legislators about what constitutes valuable learning for kids, and continuing my own professional growth as a leader and a learner are essential to making schools better. Early in the certification process, I realized that automatic pilot does not maximize instructional time and certainly does not accommodate the individual needs of the students and the school.

The National Board Certification process had a metamorphic impact on my own teaching as well as on my colleagues' practice. We began to make radical changes in our instructional practices during the process, not just after completion. It gave me the language I needed to clearly communicate to and with other teaching professionals what was best for my students and why. Aligning our practice with the standards (for what accomplished teachers should know and be able to do) helped us achieve that critical balance between content knowledge and pedagogy. It made us better teachers. This is why I recommend the National Board Certification process to educators everywhere. I know what it will do for their teaching and for their students. National Board Certification is by far the most significant influence on what I know and can do as a teaching professional. It has made me a leader. National Board Certification is not a destination; it's a journey. Leadership is the answer to the question, "After certification, what next?"

The National Board for Professional Teaching Standards is the impetus for helping teachers shape their conversations about teaching and learning and engage in professional dialogue that demonstrates what teachers and students should know and be able to do in the classroom. The five core propositions provide the knowledge base for how accomplished teaching should be defined. This definition includes commitment, knowledge, responsibility, reflection, and leadership. Accomplished teachers, those who can successfully lead the profession, are committed to students and their learning. They not only know their content but they know how to teach this to students in ways students can understand. They have a strong sense of responsibility for not only monitoring how students behave and learn but they also manage their students' growth and achievement. They reflectively analyze what they do as instructional leaders and why they do it, always modifying and maximizing what they learn through experience. And, finally, accomplished teachers are lifelong learners who can lead the teaching profession and improve schools from within.

I believe teacher leadership from the classroom is the missing piece to education reform. Teacher leadership is critical to moving U.S. education forward in these uncertain times. Teacher leaders must take a seat at the table of school change so their voices on teacher quality can be heard. As advocates for the professionalism of teaching and the need for increased student performance, we must build the profession as accomplished teachers and scholars. We must expand our roles as community leaders and education policymakers. We must improve schools from within, utilizing our expertise as teaching professionals and placing ourselves at the center of the education reform movement. As Adrienne Mack-Kirschner informs us all in this important book, "These stories represent what is happening in tens of thousands of classrooms. They hold within them the power of what could be if all teachers and schools provided opportunities for all children to experience powerful teaching and learning."

—*Cathy R. Owens, NBCT*
Director of Teacher Leadership Initiatives
The National Board for Professional Teaching Standards

Acknowledgments

Stories breathe life into statistics. At a time in education when the nation appears obsessed with scores and numbers and percentiles, we need to stop and get reacquainted with the children and the teachers behind those numbers. These are their stories, stories of powerful teaching and learning experiences. To find a publisher and an editor who believe with the author in the power of stories is a dream come true. Corwin Press and editor Faye Zucker have nurtured and encouraged and worked alongside me as we gathered stories from around the country.

And, of course, I salute the many teachers who so generously contributed their stories to this collection. Via e-mail, I traveled around the country making friends in Georgetown, Texas; Edmond, Oklahoma; Spokane, Washington; Arrowhead, New York; Tampa Bay, Florida; and close to home in California. Teachers shared much more than the stories we've included here. They've shared their excitement at being published and apologized for being "just a hack at writing!" (Mark Ellis). Dennis Hagen-Smith added editorial comment along with his story: "It provides an example of powerful student learning experiences which may not be measured on a standardized test or jammed between the covers of a scripted Open Court program." Kathleen Blake found time to write "most of the afternoon and evening" during a snowstorm when she was home nursing a broken leg. She wished me well "on the weaving, may your warp and your weft be powerful." I found a kindred spirit in Spokane with Foster Walsh's reminder that I am older than he by two years, which he softened a bit when he added, "Ah, the fifties—the best years of our lives, at least until the sixties."

During the collecting and the e-mails crisscrossing the country I was frequently reminded of how little encouragement teachers receive and how little it takes to offer encouragement—a word of praise, an acknowledgment. Stacia Smith generously replied to the notice her story would be included, "Thanks for saying that it is a keeper—you have made my Valentine's Day!" (And no added calories.) Jeanne Owens reminded me how difficult it is for teachers to find a personal moment in their very busy days. She wrote, "I'm revising on passing periods, in between lunch duty." Renée O'Brien stayed up late: "I'm a night owl, that's when I do my best writing and thinking and with three children that's the only time I have to grade papers, write lesson plans, and clean the house." Still, she wrote a story. It took Brenda Smith a while because of the "pile of stories running around in my head, wondering which one to turn into writing."

Corresponding with teachers reminded me that our lives are complex and sometimes tragic. Kathy Smith's student drowned between the time she wrote the story and the book was published. At the principal's request, she read the story at the funeral services and gave a copy to the parents. I was touched by the openness with which teachers shared their stories and their lives. I cried upon learning that Constance Rogers' daughter-in-law had died. She wrote her story because she "need[ed] something to occupy my mind."

Teachers shared their joys as well. Marcia Harris wrote to say, "I appreciate your support. Today I had a good day. My student's poetry was picked for the 5th grade Anthology of Poetry. The student wrote the poem because I told her it would be better to write her feelings instead of punching a child. The poem is powerful. It is titled, 'Tired of Being Teased.'" I e-mailed Cecilia Lozano notice her story was accepted without knowing it was her birthday. "As a coincidence, I turn 43 today! I'll look at that as a good omen in beginning this online friendship with you. I also feel very passionate in my work." Susan Brandon spoke for many when she added, "Attached is my classroom story that I hope will inspire other educators."

It seems insufficient to say thank you when I want to throw open my arms and hug every teacher, those whose stories appear within these pages and those whose stories are yet to be heard. But thank you is all I have at my disposal, so I thank you all and I salute you.

One last word of thanks goes to my husband, Stuart, who listened patiently while I read stories, who handed me tissues when I cried, who recovered files when I crashed, and who brought me hot cups of tea so I could do this important work.

About the Author

Adrienne Mack-Kirschner, EdD, NBCT, is an education consultant and speaker with vast experience as a classroom teacher, mentor, writer, literacy coach, and support provider for candidates applying for Certification through the National Board for Professional Teaching Standards (NBPTS). She developed and directed National Board support programs at the University of California, Los Angeles, and for the Los Angeles County Office of Education. She has personally supported more than 700 teachers in the certification process, enjoying one of the highest success rates in the country.

Her publications include *The Teacher's Guide to National Board Certification: Unpacking the Standards* (2003), *The National Board Certification Workbook: How to Prepare Your Portfolio* (2003), and *A+ Parents: Help Your Child Learn and Succeed in School* (1998). Her Web site is www.accomplishedteaching.com.

About the Contributors

Diane Saienni Albanese, NBCT
Early Adolescence/English Language Arts, 2001
Cape Henlopen Schools, Lewes, DE 19958

Pamela Beery, NBCT
Early Adolescence/English Language Arts, 2001
Delaware City School District, Delaware, OH 43015

Tammi Bender, NBCT
Middle Childhood/Generalist, 1998
Mayfield Schools, Mayfield, OH 44124

Kathleen A. Blake, NBCT
Early Adolescence and Adolescence & Young Adulthood/Art, 1998
Edmond Public Schools, Memorial High School, Edmond, OK 73013

Genevieve Bodnar, NBCT
Middle Childhood/Generalist, 1996
Youngstown City Schools, Youngstown, OH 44503

Susan Sheffield Brandon, NBCT
Middle Childhood/Generalist, 2001
Hillsborough County Schools, Valrico Elementary School,
Valrico, FL 33594

Kelly Campbell-Busby, NBCT
Early Through Middle Childhood/Art, 2001
Homewood City Schools, Homewood, AL 35209

Marlene Carter, NBCT
Adolescence & Young Adulthood/English Language Arts, 2000
Los Angeles Unified School District and the California
Writing Project, Los Angeles, CA 90016

Karen M. Caruso, NBCT
Early Childhood/Generalist, 2000
Third Street Elementary School, Los Angeles, CA 90004

Judith A. Chalmers, NBCT
Early Childhood/Generalist, 2001
Oklahoma City Public Schools, Coolidge Elementary School,
Oklahoma City, OK 73013

Sharon Chaney, NBCT
Adolescence & Young Adulthood/English Language Arts, 1999
Hunters Lane High School, Nashville, TN 37207

Odessa Cleveland, NBCT
Early Adolescence/English Language Arts, 2000
Peer Assistance and Review Program (LAUSD/UTLA),
Los Angeles, CA 90010

William A. Dean, NBCT
Adolescence & Young Adulthood/English Language Arts, 2000
East Palo Alto High School, Menlo Park, CA 94025

John Dorroh, NBCT
Adolescence & Young Adulthood/Science, 1999
Mississippi Writing/Thinking Institute, Mississippi State University,
Mississippi State, MS 39762

Mark W. Ellis, NBCT
Early Adolescence/Mathematics, 1999
University of North Carolina, Chapel Hill, NC 27599

Alfee Enciso, NBCT
Adolescence & Young Adulthood/English Language Arts, 1999
Los Angeles Unified School District,
Los Angeles, CA, 90023

Patrice J. Faison, NBCT
Early Childhood/Generalist, 2000
North Carolina Agricultural and Technical State University,
Greensboro, NC 27411

David Feela, NBCT
Adolescence & Young Adulthood/English Language Arts, 1982
Montezuma-Cortez School District RE-1, Cortez, CO 81321

Marta C. Findlay-Partridge, NBCT
Early Adolescence Through Young Adulthood/Music, 2002
Wake County Schools, Raleigh, NC 27606

Rosemary Fryer, NBCT
Adolescence & Young Adulthood/English Language Arts, 2001
Evergreen School District 114, Heritage High School,
Vancouver, WA 98685

Kathryn R. Gemmer, NBCT
Adolescence & Young Adulthood/Science, 2001
University School, East Tennessee State University,
Johnson City, TN 37614

Kathleen Ann González, NBCT
Adolescence & Young Adulthood/English Language Arts, 2000
Santa Teresa High School, San Jose, CA 95123

Anthony John Vincent Griffin, NBCT candidate
Early Childhood/Generalist, 2002/2003
Compton Unified School District, Compton, CA 90220

Wendy Hacke, NBCT
Early Childhood/Generalist, 2002
Alum Rock Union School District/National Hispanic University,
San Jose, CA 95127

Mary Marshall Hanson, NBCT
Middle Childhood/Generalist, 2003
Pasadena Unified School District, Pasadena, CA 91109

Marcia L. Harris, NBCT candidate
Middle Childhood/Generalist, 2002/2003
ABC Unified School District, Cerritos, CA 90703

Olivia Herring, NBCT
Early Adolescence/English Language Arts, 2001
Los Angeles Unified School District, Hollenbeck Middle School, Los
Angeles, CA 90023

Janet H. Hironaka, NBCT
Early Adolescence/English Language Arts, 1998
Los Angeles Unified School District, District K, Gardena, CA 90247

Helene Hirsch, NBCT candidate
Early Adolescence/English Language Arts, 2003
Holmes Middle School, Northridge, CA 91325

Linda C. Hollett, NBCT
Early and Middle Childhood/Art, 2002
Henrico County Public Schools, Richmond, VA 23228

Catherine Humphrey, PhD, NBCT
Adolescence and Young Adulthood/English Language Arts, 2000
Los Osos High School, Alta Loma, CA 91737

Linda T. Johnson, NBCT
Early Childhood/Specialist, 2001
Bount County Board of Education, Oneonta, AL 35121

Joel Kammer, NBCT
Adolescence & Young Adulthood/English Language Arts, 2002
Maria Carrillo High School, Santa Rosa, CA 95409

Barbara Yvette LeWinter, NBCT
Middle Childhood/Generalist, 1998
Los Angeles Unified School District, Van Nuys, CA 91405

Cecilia D. Lozano, NBCT candidate
Adolescence & Young Adulthood/English Language Arts, 2003
Oklahoma City Public Schools, Southeast High School,
Oklahoma City, OK 73129

Christina Maffia, NBCT
Middle Childhood/Generalist, 1999
Three Village School District, East Setauket, NY 11733

Cheri J. Mann, former NBCT candidate
Eminence High School, Eminence, KY 40019

Sharon McCubbin, NBCT
Middle Childhood/Generalist, 2000
Early Through Middle Childhood/ English as a New Language, 2002
Irvine Unified School District, Irvine, CA 92620

Renee A. Moore, NBCT
Adolescence & Young Adulthood/English Language Arts, 2001
North Bolivar School District, Shelby, MS 38774

Carolyn Moser, NBCT
Early Adolescence/Science, 2002
Wake County Public Schools, Raleigh, NC 27613

Renée O'Brien, NBCT
Early Adolescence/Generalist, 2000
Pinellas County School District, Bay Point Middle School,
St. Petersburg, FL 33712

Nicki O'Neill, NBCT
Early Childhood/Exceptional Needs Specialist, 2002
Saint Lucie County School Board, Port Saint Lucie, FL 34953

Jeanne Owens, NBCT
Early Adolescence/English Language Arts, 2002
Muskogee Public School, Muskogee, OK 74401

Lynn Gannon Patterson, EdD, NBCT
Middle Childhood/Generalist, 1998
Homer Pittard Campus School, Murfreesboro, TN 37132

Stephanie Penniman, NBCT
Middle Childhood/Generalist, 2000
Los Angeles Unified School District, Plummer Street Elementary
School, North Hills, CA 91343

Kathleen Pickard, NBCT candidate
Early Childhood/Generalist, 2002/2003
Charter Oak Unified School District, Covina, CA 91723

Damien Riley, NBCT candidate
Middle Childhood/English Language Arts, 2003
Adelanto School District, Westside Park Elementary School,
Adelanto, CA 92307

Maureen Robinson, NBCT
Early Adolescence/Social Studies-History, 2002
Osceola County School District, Parkway Middle School,
Kissimmee, FL 34743

Constance M. Rogers, NBCT
Early and Middle Childhood/Art, 2002
Walton School District, Van R. Butler Elementary School,
Santa Rosa Beach, FL 32459

David Ross, NBCT
Middle Childhood/Generalist, 2003
Fernangeles Elementary School, Sun Valley, CA 91352

Macre Jay Schwartz, NBCT
Early Childhood Through Young Adult/Exceptional Needs
Specialist, 2002
Pasadena Unified School District, Pasadena, CA 91109

Ann Matthys Smalley, NBCT
Early Childhood/Generalist, 2001
Austin Independent Schools, Austin, TX 78757

Brenda Culp Smith, NBCT
Adolescence & Young Adulthood/English Language Arts, 2000
Newton-Conover High School, Newton, NC 28658

Kathy L. Smith, NBCT
Early Adolescence/English Language Arts, 2002
Lake County School Board, Carver Middle School,
Leesburg, FL 34748

Stacia A. Smith, PhD, NBCT
Early Adolescence/English Language Arts, 1997
Dayton Public Schools, Associate Superintendent,
Dayton, OH 45417

Shelia D. Sutton, MA, NBCT
Early Adolescence/English Language Arts, 2002
The Write Approach, Inc., Pasadena, CA 91101

Claudia L. Swisher, NBCT
Adolescence & Young Adulthood/English Language Arts, 2000
Norman North High School, Norman, OK 73069

Cindy Taylor, NBCT
Early Adolescence/English Language Arts, 2001
Spartanburg School District, Spartanburg, SC 29307

Michael Taylor, NBCT
Early Adolescence/English Language Arts, 2002
Pinellas County School District, St. Petersburg, FL, 33712

Foster Walsh, NBCT
Adolescence & Young Adulthood/English Language Arts, 2001
Gonzaga University, Spokane, WA 99258

Rebecca L. Witt, NBCT
Early Childhood Through Young Adulthood/Exceptional
Needs Specialist, 2001
Collier County Public Schools, Naples, FL 34104

Introduction

The Power of Story

The idea for this book began in . . .

No, allow me to begin again—the compelling need for this collection of stories from the classroom began knocking on my soul in the late 1990s, shortly after I was touched by the names on the AIDS quilt circulating throughout the nation. The power of those names and dates embroidered and painted on the quilt brought life to the statistics announcing the number of lives cut short by AIDS. If names and dates had the power to transform flat statistics to lives touched, then imagine the power that would flow from stories behind each of those names.

In the fall of 2002 an exhibit of life-size photos of people associated with the 9/11 attack on New York's World Trade Center toured the country. I viewed the exhibit at the Skirball Center in Los Angeles. The curators had left boxes of facial tissues strewn generously beneath and beside the photos. Accompanying each photo was a short paragraph, words from the firefighters and nurses, the police officers, and corporate executives. Men and women, young and old were touched by the stories more deeply than we had been impressed by the numbers totaling the dead and missing. The power of stories again.

In December 2002, I visited Ellis Island in New York. That exhibit in its entirety tells the story of tens of thousands of hopeful immigrants coming to America, and the wall of memory where my grandparents' names are etched brought them to life for me; nothing was more memorable than the individual stories told on audiotapes and film. The power of stories.

Every culture in every time has used story to record its history, to memorialize heroes, to eternalize events, to reinforce roles, and to aid understanding. Stories teach our children about our morals and our traditions. Teachers, secular and religious, in formal and informal settings, tell stories. Perhaps it is because we have moved away from storytelling that we've become more disconnected from our children. Yet, you need only begin a conversation with, "Let me tell you a story," to have everyone's attention.

This book is about our stories, stories told by classroom teachers, stories that reach behind and around and under the statistics to bring the art and craft of teaching to life. These stories breathe life into the children and teachers who fill our classrooms. These stories must be told.

Charles Dickens began one of his most famous and important stories with the seemingly contradictory line, "It was the best of times, it was the worst of times." Bear with me while I join the hundreds who have borrowed this line. It is the best of times in education—never before has education been of such high priority at every government level, local to international. Never before has the stated intention in the United States been to educate every child, black, brown, and white, rich or poor, to the highest level of which they are capable.

It is also the worst of times in education. Every day, it seems, policymakers at the national, state, district, or school level issue edicts declaring what curriculum should be taught, to whom it will be taught, and how it will be taught. There's been an increased call for *standardization,* for *teacher-proof* scripted lessons, for lock-step scope and sequences, and for pacing plans. Equal opportunity is equated to *sameness* of input, as if putting the same thing into each child will result in getting the same thing out—higher test scores. The policymakers act as if children are the tabula rasas teachers are mandated to fill up so they can regurgitate the stipulated facts on state achievement tests so the school and district in turn look good and property values rise and the mandates of the federal No Child Left Behind Act leave the schools alone. But there's a disconnection here. Socioeconomics aren't children, data about years of teaching don't reflect effectiveness, and test scores represent only a small piece of what children learn in schools.

While the debates about testing, which tests, how often, and how many, circulate, accomplished teachers moan to themselves and to like-minded colleagues. They quietly close their classroom doors and continue to teach groups of children, respectfully treating each child as if he or she were their only charge. They employ effective teaching strategies they know from experience and from continuous observation result in powerful learning. But they perform their artistry in private, much like Emily Dickinson wrote her poetry. Art needs audience. In order to impact education policy, we need to open those doors so that those who make the external decisions can see the children and the teachers, in Grades pre-K through 12, across all content areas, throughout the nation, who make magical things happen. Stories are deliciously rich in bringing the abstract to life, of changing the nameless, faceless children into precious beings filled with potential.

All of our lives have been touched by the teachers who have taught us. I've been fortunate to have had some wonderful teachers whose lessons continue to influence my life. While I can't remember any of the questions, and would probably have difficulty recalling many of the facts that appeared on the required New York State Regents exams I had to pass before graduating from Jamaica High School in 1960, I do remember what I learned in sixth grade:

- How to get along with others
- Respect my classmates
- Kindness is powerful
- How to sew using the combination stitch
- What a hair looks like under a microscope
- And I learned not to sing

Now let me tell you a story about sixth grade . . .

It's Okay Not to Be Perfect

Adrienne Mack-Kirschner

Sixth-grade lessons come in many guises. I went to school during the 1950s when girls wore full skirts and crinolines to class. One day when walking to the front of the room to deliver some papers to the teacher sitting at her desk, my crinoline slipped from under my skirt and fell in folds around my ankles—the victim of a missing button. While I stood there frozen, Mrs. Mecklenberg told me to step out of the slip, pick it up, and go to the restroom. She sent another student after me with buttons and safety pins. I made the repair, but feared returning to class. After lingering as long as I could in the girl's room, I ventured timidly into the classroom. To my astonishment, not one child said anything. There was no laughter or teasing, not in class and not in the playground or after school. Not one child ever mentioned the mishap. You can't measure what I learned in Mrs. Mecklenberg's class on a standardized test, but you can see the lessons playing out in my life every day. In sixth grade I learned about the importance of a safe learning environment and how safety means much more than just freedom from physical violence. Today I look a lot more like Mrs. Mecklenberg than like the 11-year-old with the fallen crinoline I once was, but she's still my teacher. I remember that little girl and the teacher who made it okay not to be perfect but to be a continuous work in progress.

Unfortunately, not all teachers were like Mrs. Mecklenberg. During the same year a visiting music teacher came one Friday morning and instructed the sixth graders to sing rounds of *Three Blind Mice*. We sang round after round while she circulated, her ear close to our open mouths, listening to the sounds coming out. When she tapped me on the shoulder, one of the few chosen ones, I sang even louder. I loved to sing, as did my father. Singing was joyous and filled with possibilities—both especially important to a child growing up in a government housing project. When she had completed evaluating all of the students she returned to the front of the room. *Will those students whom I tapped*, I held my breath self-consciously expecting praise, *not sing. You're off key and you ruin the songs for everyone else.* I can recall the exact moment when I stopped singing. Nearly four decades passed before I found my voice again. It was still off-key, but perfect pitch is not what singing is all about. I take the lessons I learned in school and carry them to my own classrooms where I attempt to transform them for my own students. That is the power of story.

In seventh grade at Parsons Junior High School our New Age English teacher wore beads and let her hair hang loose. She sat cross-legged dangerously close to the edge of her desk; our attention was riveted probably as much by her pose as by her words. In our class we didn't just read books, our teacher taught us to talk with the authors. *If you have something to say to the authors, if you want to tell them how their words touched or surprised or angered you, then tell them.* We filled the margins of the books we read with penciled-in commentary. We read our classmates' marginalia and wrote back. Discussions were rich and deep and meaningful. We were part of a learning community of readers and writers, conspiring together to make meaning from the texts we read. My conversations with authors didn't end in seventh grade. I prowled used bookstores in Greenwich Village so I could purchase and own books that I could continue to write in. My home bookshelves are filled with thousands of volumes, all friends of mine. They're combination books and journals at the same time. I'm 12 years old, or 20, or 43 again when I reread the marginalia and comment on my own comments. My life as a writer began in seventh grade.

I can change modes here and tell you about my teaching theory. I can stress the importance of standards, of high expectations for all students, of holding everyone accountable, or I can tell you another story, a story about one of my students, whose name was Maria.

As Loud as Thunder

Adrienne Mack-Kirschner

From the first day of school, my high school freshmen English students know that by the end of the year they each will need to demonstrate proficiency in the domains of reading, writing, listening, and speaking. My mission during the first weeks of school includes uncovering students' strengths as well as the areas where they will benefit from more focused assistance. Some students are challenged by writing effectively; others by comprehending the texts they encounter in core classes. All of them have difficulty applying active listening skills. And then there are those students, like Maria, who have progressed satisfactorily by completing homework and passing tests, but whose voices remain silent. Because the ability to work collaboratively and to present one's ideas is increasingly valued in the workplace, helping students to find their voices is critically important, even though verbal skills are not measured on conventional tests.

Fifteen-year-old Maria was a master at avoiding attention in class. She never raised her hand. Even when I knew from reading her essays and journals that she had valuable insights to contribute to class discussions, she chose silence. In groups, she volunteered to record rather than to present. I thought of the itinerant music teacher who had stolen my voice and vowed to assist Maria in finding hers. We began by preparing and rehearsing answers in advance, which she delivered, still seated, at a prearranged signal. Slowly she progressed to joining in group presentations in which she would not have to face the class alone. During her first group presentation, she knew she'd disappointed her teammates when the other students couldn't hear her report due to the softness of her voice. Her frustration doubled her determination to be heard. Throughout the semester we worked on speaking publicly, progressing from responding when called upon to raising her hand and offering an opinion. However, it wasn't until nearly the end of the spring term that Maria gave the performance neither she nor I would ever forget.

The assignment was to memorize a poem and present it to the class the way a poet might. It wasn't until I read her year-end portfolio that I understood how important Maria's presentation was to her. She wrote about how nervous she was standing alone in front of the class and how suddenly, as she was reciting the poem, she realized that she didn't care about anything except pronouncing the words correctly. Her voice was, according to Maria, *as loud as thunder.* She forgot three lines, but she vowed to herself then that even though she was nervous, she would still let herself be heard. *Never again,* Maria continued in her reflection, *will I talk to an audience like a little mouse, but like a big thunderstorm that nobody will want to ignore.*

I watch for students like Maria; students who silently walk the halls of our large urban schools; students who become invisible mice behind the walls. Maria trusted me and her classmates. She knew we were her partners in our classroom learning community. As her teacher I had worked first to make the classroom a safe place to take risks, something I had learned from my sixth-grade teacher. Only because she felt safe was she able to grow. When she finished reciting her poem—the title of which escapes me—there were tears rolling down my cheeks. Her classmates cheered while Maria remained standing behind the podium, smiling. That morning I remembered why I had chosen teaching as a profession.

What follows in these pages are stories from teachers who raise their students, like Maria, to higher levels, adding value to their lives, not just in reading, writing, and arithmetic, but as citizens of the world.

For this first collection of stories, we've chosen to call upon National Board Certified Teachers (NBCTs) and candidates for certification because as an NBCT myself I knew that they had spent months reflecting on their teaching in preparation for completing the portfolio entries required by the National Board for Professional Teaching Standards (NBPTS). If you are not already familiar with the NBPTS, I encourage you to go to their Web site and learn about National Board Certification and what it might hold for you and for the teachers you know and work with. The National Board for Professional Teaching Standards, calling upon the best teachers, researchers, educators, and community members from around the nation, identified the five essential ingredients found in the most effective classrooms. I used these principles to organize the stories that follow:

- Teachers are committed to students and their learning.
- Teachers know the subjects they teach and how to teach those subjects so students can learn.
- Teachers are responsible for managing and monitoring student learning.
- Teachers think systematically about their practice and learn from experience.
- Teachers are members of learning communities.

But in reality, once the call for stories had gone out through all the e-mails and listservs I belonged to, and once the stories began to arrive, we realized that they are deeply complex and defy rigid categorization. Just like good lessons, they don't address just one standard, but weave their way throughout the propositions and could just as easily fit in one chapter as in another. Therefore, I ask you to be flexible and to consider the big picture, not just the specific proposition that heads each chapter.

This collection is offered to inspire you, to remind you why you chose to become a teacher and why you remain one. It is my hope that policymakers at every level will learn from these pages what powerful teaching and learning are all about. The stories will move you beyond the data analysis and beyond the published test scores that affect real estate prices without regard to the lives of children and their teachers. I read the stories as they arrived, frequently reading them aloud to my husband. Some drew tears, others laughter, until my husband jokingly complained that there weren't enough tissues in the house for me to write this book. I ignored him, grabbed another box of tissues, and kept reading. I hope you will also.

Take the stories to the faculty lounge or the legislative analyst's office, read them to one another, or in book clubs, or at PTA meetings. Remember that the students we're collectively responsible for are first children, not receptacles into which we dump information. These are young people needing to learn respect, self-confidence, the habits of learning and thinking and compassion. The future is sitting in today's classrooms. Our students are the hope for the world, and you, as teachers and supporters of teachers, are charged with growing compassionate world citizens capable of fostering and continuing democracy.

RESOURCE

The National Board for Professional Teaching Standards. http://www.nbpts.org

Teachers Are Committed to Students and Their Learning

My students are always surprised when I share with them how nervous I am on the first day of school. Who's going to come into my classroom? What will they think of me? Will they like me? Will they think I'm smart? Will I be a good enough teacher to teach each of them? My students are surprised because they have the same questions about their teachers that we have about our students. Those students who have had good experiences enter our classrooms joyfully. Others, who have experienced failure, sometimes come reluctantly. Students who have experienced school failure come to your room hoping that this year will be different. They all come wanting their teachers to teach them well.

Since we teach our students based upon what we believe about them, we must begin our practice by examining our beliefs and by ensuring that we do embrace the premise that all students can learn. No matter what our explanation for poor student performance, student achievement is dependent primarily upon us. The quality of the teaching is the single most important factor in a child's education. "All researchers agree that the impact of decisions made by individual teachers is far greater than the impact of decisions made at the school level" (Marzano, 2003, p. 85).

The teachers whose stories are in this collection "not only recognize that students have individual differences, they seek out those differences, build on them, and find ways to use those differences to make content meaningful" (Mack-Kirschner, 2003, p. 87). These teachers look past student appearance and dress, even past some of the less socially acceptable mannerisms students may adopt as a mechanism to survive in their environment. We don't identify students by single characteristics. Students are not just the "Ritalin kid," or the one in the wheelchair, or the foster kid. Accomplished teachers are vigilant about seeing the whole child. They find something loveable about every child who enters the classroom.

Teachers are missionaries, parents, mentors, and friends, even before we're academics. Our students are native born and immigrant. They are the huddled masses of Emma Lazarus's poem on the Statue of Liberty, "yearning to breathe free." Teachers are the breath of democracy for many students. We carry our students in our hearts, feed them from our pockets, and take them into our homes. Students feed our souls, and we feast on all they give us. This is where it all begins. These stories remind me, as they will you, of the awesome responsibility a teacher has. We make a difference in students' lives. In what other profession can a simple phrase turn a life around? Christina Maffia's story is the story of every teacher who sets out to touch a life.

Making a Difference

Christina Maffia

Three days before the beginning of school I was appointed to a teaching position as a fourth-grade teacher in the lowest tracked class in a New York City classroom. This was my childhood dream. I'd envisioned I would grow up and save humanity. But that dream turned into a nightmare as I felt I had been thrown into shark-infested waters to sink or swim. During those first few weeks I was drowning. Nevertheless, without books or supplies I set out to change the world and make a difference in the lives of my students. I had great ideas and could not wait to share my lessons and knowledge with them. What I did not realize in those early days was how much *they* would teach me and how *they* would change my life.

So, it was during the first week of school that I planned to read Aesop's fables. Prior to reading *The Country Mouse and the City Mouse*, I created a Venn diagram and had the class brainstorm the similarities and differences of city life and country life. I carefully recorded their answers on chart paper in the two interlocking circles. Riyad raised his hand. "Miss," as he referred to me, "cows live in the city." "Oh no Riyad, cows do not live in the city," was my prompt reply and I immediately called upon the next raised hand. Again, Riyad waved his hand and when I responded he most respectfully told me that cows live in the city. Again I dismissed his remarks, calling upon another raised hand. Ever-persistent, Riyad raised his hand yet a third time and said, "Miss, cows live in the city." Frustrated I asked, "What city are you referring to, Riyad?" "In my country, Miss, in Guyana." At that moment the lightbulb went off over my head! That was the beginning of a lifelong lesson this student taught me that autumn day. In order for me to become an accomplished and effective teacher, I needed to get to know my students, not just assess their learning within the classroom. I needed to learn about their culture, their needs, wants, desires, to know about their lives outside the classroom.

I set out to learn more about Riyad, both academically and per-sonally. Riyad's reading and comprehension skills were substantially below grade level, yet his work ethic was strong and his desire to achieve even stronger. Assessing his strengths and weaknesses was my first priority and with long hours spent working together, Riyad improved in all subject areas. Piecing together the information I learned about him over time gave me some insight to the financial struggles that he, his mother, and sister were facing. I offered support to his mother through gifts of food and outgrown clothing from my children. In time Riyad and his family became our adopted family and spent Christmas with us.

Through the years Riyad called often to report on his school suc-cesses. Hardships and sacrifices have permeated his life. He and his family lived in a two-room basement apartment that floods with each rainfall. Living with the fear of eviction knocking on their door has not been easy, yet they persevere. Of the 38,000 underprivileged high school seniors he was chosen as one of 350 semifinalists for the prestigious *New York Times* scholarship. Senior year he achieved his elementary-school goal of becoming the valedictorian.

Recently, he asked if I would take him to his Harvard interview. On our car ride there he told me of the impact I had on his school success, but I reminded him that it was his hard work and dedication that made him successful, not me. That 9-year-old's persistence still shone through when he replied, "But Miss, you were the one who taught me that I always had to do my best to achieve my goals. Don't you remember the day when Joseph, a classmate, asked you why you had chosen me to be Student of the Week? You told him because I always worked so hard. After you spoke those words I knew I could never disappoint you. And that has made all the difference in my life." Glancing at him in the rearview mirror, I almost had to pull the car off the road when my teary vision blurred.

A decade ago in that New York City classroom, I vowed to make a difference and positively impact the lives of my students. I never thought that they would make a difference in mine, but they continue to enrich me daily.

Accomplished teachers are amazing people. We believe we can add *value* to every child who walks through our door, even those others have given up on. I'm not certain it's not mostly about the stubborn streak that runs through us, or maybe it is the missionary we alluded to in Christina's story. Whatever the reason, students who are fortunate enough to have one or more of these amazing teachers in their lives gain much more than what can be taken from a textbook. Teachers also are blessed in many ways by the students they teach. I've always been attracted to the underdogs and the misfits, and to those who challenge the status quo like the children Renee Moore writes about. Not all of our students win scholarships or become class valedictorians. Sometimes we're not able to save every child or divert them from the path they are on. The fact that we don't always succeed doesn't justify not trying. Renee Moore reaffirms her reasons for teaching every time she is able to touch a child's life.

Christopher and Clarence

Renee A. Moore

Over the course of my teaching career, I have received many awards, but few were as precious or as instructive as were students Christopher and Clarence. When I met Christopher, he was 18 years old and walking into my 10th-grade English class after having spent his entire school career in a self-contained special education class. His mother had decided that she wanted Chris, the last of her seven children, to graduate from high school with a diploma. He was actually pretty good in math and some other subjects, but had severe problems in reading and writing. Chris could not write a coherent sentence. He may have been dyslexic, but at that time our small rural school district had no testing or provisions to determine the problem or way to treat learning disabilities. I taught Christopher for 2 years in a row. His mother, older sister, and I were determined to help him to pass the state mandatory functional literacy examination.

This was a young man who had been written off as hopeless by so many people and for so long that even he didn't believe he could actually learn. He sat quietly, sitting to one side of the classroom, writing by himself while I worked with the rest of the class. His writing was painstakingly slow, and he made all sorts of facial contortions as he struggled to put together even simple sentences. By the end of the first year with me he could write a decent paragraph. By the end of the second year, he was ready to tackle the reading and written communication sections of the test. It took three attempts, but he finally did pass.

Clarence, on the other hand, presented a whole different set of challenges. By ninth grade he had already embarked on a life of crime, right after his best friend, who was also a student in my ninth-grade English class that year, shot himself through the head. I watched as 17-year-old Clarence's already weak foundation crumpled into full-fledged self-destruction. Then, one Friday afternoon, while the rest of the student body poured into the gym around 2:30 for a pep rally, Clarence begged me to help him write an essay. I remember staring at this disheveled, hollow-eyed kid who had spent the previous weekend in jail, was currently on probation (which was the only reason he came to school), and skipped every class except P.E. and mine, and heard myself saying, "Sure, what do you want to write about?"

We worked until almost 5 P.M. I don't even remember the topic now, only that he asked me to pick one. What he really wanted was to prove, mostly to himself, that he could write one. When we finished, he sat there grinning. He asked me to keep it. I didn't see Clarence again for a few days. When he did return, he asked for his essay and sat in the back of class copying it. He handed me the original as he left the room. After that, he was in and out of school, until finally I heard he'd been arrested again. Clarence is in state prison now. We write to one another, my attempt at keeping the promise alive.

There have been lots of Christophers and some Clarences in my teaching life. Some of the stories have happy endings, some have sadder ones, and some endings have yet to be written. Taken together, they are blessings for which I am deeply grateful and the reason I love what God has called me to do.

I'm a worrier. I worry about everything and everyone. My father used to tease me about my propensity for worrying. "Why are you trying to take God's job?" he'd ask. "Let God do the worrying." I heard him, but I didn't listen. Now it's my husband who complains that some nights the sound of my thinking keeps him awake. I worry most about students who are not receiving a high quality education, who are in reductive environments void of quality verbal discourse. So much of what we do in school, especially at the secondary level, is irrelevant at a time when it needn't be and shouldn't be. I don't think there's ever been a time as exciting as this; new information arrives moment by moment. We can't afford to lose any children because we don't convincingly demonstrate the value of education and the importance of what we are teaching and expect students to learn.

In an article in the *Christian Science Monitor* that appeared on March 4, 2003, Helana Kadyszewski reported a University of Michigan's Institute for Social Research study confirming that only 28% of high school seniors consider their schoolwork "often or always meaningful," down from 40% 20 years earlier. Only 21% thought their courses were "quite or very interesting," dropping 14% in 20 years. And we're not talking only about students who are turned off to school, "Even among A-students, fewer and fewer forecast that their schoolwork will be very important later in life . . . [and these results] were largely independent of the type of high school program—academic, vocational, or technical—the students were enrolled in" (Kadyszewski, 2003).

Accomplished teachers are proactive. They find ways to make connections for students and they ensure the curriculum relates to students' lives, to their interests, and to their futures. When Paul came to Carolyn Moser's middle school Science classroom, he was already failing several classes. He just wouldn't do what wasn't within his interest zone. The teacher helped Paul to expand his interest zone and to see the relevance in what he was being asked to do. The teacher turned this potential dropout into a college-bound electrical engineering student.

The Hook

Carolyn Moser

The first day I met Paul, I knew that he was an exceptional boy. That proved to be very true. As a middle school Science teacher, I have become very skilled in recognizing students who have that special spark that sets them apart. They are the students who ask questions that never occur to you and who have a curiosity that's never satisfied. I knew instantly that Paul was one of these special students who would set the world on fire.

Unfortunately, Paul was one of many students who was very bright and creative, but had great difficulty in disciplining himself to do the things in school that were not within his interest zone. He hated to write and found homework assignments too much trouble and boring. While Paul had an above-average intelligence, he was failing three subjects. He was frustrated and so were his parents. We were fearful that Paul would join the ranks of students who "fell through the cracks" in school because he failed to see the importance of all areas of the curriculum.

Because Paul loved science, I had a definite advantage in trying to change the way he perceived school, teachers, and homework. Paul loved electronics. I took this interest and searched for topics that might interest him. He was like a sponge whenever I gave him a book or a magazine that had information about science. He stayed after school to work on special science projects. I'd work at my desk, meet with other teachers, and do the countless other things that occupy teachers' time, while Paul would putter around my Science classroom working on his projects. When he had a question and wanted to talk about what he was doing, I stopped and spent time talking with him about whatever he might be working on at that particular time. I learned as much as Paul did as we pondered over books, trying to figure out how things worked. I also got to know Paul very well. This routine continued for months, until I suggested that Paul enter the regional science fair. He liked the idea so we began preparing a project.

During these hours after school, Paul and I had time to talk about lots of things. He told me about his other classes and why he just could not seem to do the assignments that he thought were dull and monotonous. I asked Paul to bring his books after school and we looked at the assignments. I gradually helped Paul to see that the assignments were not meaningless. If he had to write a paper, he could use his knowledge of science to write the paper. We looked at the math homework. I showed Paul that he was doing the same mathematical processes while he worked on his science fair project. He slowly began to see the connections between what he was doing in Science class and the other subjects that he did not enjoy. I explained to Paul that in order to reach the levels that he wanted to reach in life, he would have to complete classes in other subjects besides Science. Together we made a game of doing the homework, trying to find connections to science wherever we could. Paul's grades improved and so did his attitude toward school. Those afternoons working in my classroom showed Paul that there is a purpose in all learning even when we cannot readily recognize that purpose. Paul won the regional science fair that year before his family moved away. I lost touch with him and his family.

Years passed until one day I was sitting at my desk on a Friday afternoon when I heard a knock on the door. I turned and saw a tall boy. No introduction was necessary. I knew the boy was Paul. He told me that he had been accepted at one of the top universities in our state. He'd graduated from high school with honors and was looking at a wonderful future in college where he would major in electrical engineering. Paul came by to say thank you for believing in him and for redirecting his life. He gave me a hug as we said good-bye and we promised to keep in touch. I knew that Paul would find success in life. His success was my success. Being a special person in the life of a child is my greatest joy as a teacher.

Sometimes we bond with a student and then circumstances arise that take the child out of our class. Our teaching lives are so hectic, it's difficult to keep track of students who pass in, then out, and who are then replaced with another group whose own needs draw on our attention. Although we usually welcome every child, sometimes a student is preceded by her reputation, and if it's not a good one, we brace ourselves, anticipating a difficult year. Kathleen Pickard knew Mona by reputation long before she became her teacher.

Oh No, Not Her!

Kathleen Pickard

Each year our class rosters are posted a few weeks before school begins, and it is usually the teachers' first glimpse of their students. After reading my roster and noting that Mona was to be in my class, colleagues expressed sympathy, followed by their own relief in knowing Mona wouldn't be in any of their classes. Those who had encountered Mona before quietly rolled their eyes. Hers was one of the few names I recognized, and it was not because of complimentary stories that I recognized her name. I feared what the year held for my class and for me, but I made up my mind to downplay the negative that had been thrown my way.

In the first days of school Mona surpassed the rumors that preceded her. She challenged me beyond any experience I had yet acquired. She was clearly a capable child, but her behavior interfered with her academic journey. Finding ways to help her work to her potential while meeting the needs of 19 other students became a constant challenge. Mona was the first child who'd ever blatantly ignored class routines. Her behaviors included walking out of the classroom and loudly telling me she would not cooperate. When I was sure I couldn't stand another day of academics lost to Mona's behavior, I decided to videotape her so that I could begin to find answers to my concerns and prepare solutions. National Board release forms in hand, I set up a video camera for 3 days. I told my class that it was to help them get used to a camera in the classroom, while secretly I taped Mona. I learned so much about Mona and about myself through viewing and reflecting upon what I saw in those tapes, and with the camera running I was able to help bring peace to my classroom while helping Mona work to her potential. Through simple adjustments made from observing the video, I was able to assign Mona positions of responsibility at key transitional points throughout the day. I was amazed at the huge change in her behavior. One of the most effective strategies with Mona involved two behavior journals. One journal, the one Mona handled, focused only on her positive behavior. Although there were days when it was a stretch of the imagination to find a positive, I always found something to write in it. Mona's grandmother told me that Mona often stood at the door waiting excitedly to share her journal when her grandmother came home from work. The second journal was a log of her unacceptable behaviors intended strictly for conversation with her grandparents, who are her guardians. Unfortunately Mona moved, and I was not able to have the full impact for which I'd hoped. However, the lessons I learned from my interactions with Mona will last throughout my teaching career and impact many students who come to my classroom to learn.

Kathleen's story about Mona (I've changed the student's name) could have ended when Mona transferred to another setting, but it didn't. Kathleen had learned so much about Mona that she wanted to pass that knowledge along to the next teacher—whoever that might be. How many of us have worked successfully with a student, only to have that same student pass to another teacher and then fall back into old behaviors? Kathleen didn't want that to happen. Instead of saying that Mona was now someone else's problem, she took the time to write the following letter, which I encouraged her to share with all of us.

To Whom This May Concern,

I am writing on behalf of Mona White. I am her current second grade teacher, and she will be moving in two days. This will take her out of my class and put her into yours. I am hoping that the things I have discovered in the past three weeks will help you to go forward with Mona and help avoid a setback.

The first days with Mona in my class were very hard. In fact there were moments of complete and total frustration. Mona can be rude, defiant, and difficult to say the least. By the end of the first week I was sure that I could not survive a year with her. During the second week I recognized a need to come up with some significant intervention because I was sure nobody in my class could learn with Mona's behavior constantly interfering. As luck would have it, I had permission from Mona's grandparents to videotape her for my National Board portfolio. I decided to set up a video camera in the classroom to help me understand the situation and find solutions. I learned that Mona's unacceptable behavior was not as constant as I had thought. I learned some of the things that triggered Mona to act out, and most importantly, I learned that my class was indeed learning in spite of what I had believed. Now, at the end of the third week, I know Mona is reachable, I know she is loveable, and I am positive she is teachable in a classroom full of other students. I hope my findings will help you to find your way with Mona so that she can grow to her fullest potential.

I rotate my students in a complicated seating arrangement daily. Although it is difficult for students at first, it has tremendous value. While the details of my seating are not important, Mona's reaction is significant. During the first days she protested incredibly to the rotation. She insisted on sitting in the same seat as she had on the first day of school and each morning ran to the seat she had sat in the day before. Recognizing the value of my seating arrangement, I did not give in to Mona's protests and made her move to the correct table each day. Eventually Mona found a way to cope with the seating rotation. She decided to comply;

however, I noticed that her compliance involved a compromise. Each seat is numbered for cooperative jobs that change according to a job wheel after students have chosen their seat for the day. I noticed that Mona chose seat number three at each table, and she has not veered from that since the first day of school. Since jobs are chosen after students are seated, I am certain that her motives have not been driven by a desire to get a particular job. By my insisting that Mona participate in the seating rotation, Mona was able to rise to the expectation. However, allowing her to have the number three seat at each table paved the road for that success. Success for Mona requires compromise, and I found it important to recognize that Mona is trying to cope with issues in her own life. The need for compromise is not a manipulative tactic on her part.

Sharing other space in the classroom, particularly chairs, is another tough expectation for Mona to accept. It is extremely important for her to know there will be a chair for her when I work with small groups. This was very evident during Math class when I worked with small groups of children as they finished their math. Mona insisted on getting "her" chair before anyone else. This often resulted in her racing for a chair even when her math was incomplete. One day the battle over the incomplete math and chair ended with Mona walking out of the classroom without permission. Our compromise has involved me allowing Mona to sit next to me during independent math time. The result has been a more compliant little girl who completes her math. Had she remained in my room for the year, one of my long-term goals would have been to get Mona to work at her own seat during independent math time. I am completely confident that she would have met my expectations.

Walking in line can sometimes be a challenge for Mona. She often harasses the other students, and a variety of other surprises occur as well. I have learned to walk backwards, to check her frequently, and to speak to the entire class consistently about my expectations. Once again, compromise is involved. Mona will often walk out of line and reach for my hand. She needs that reassurance, and allowing it has brought peace to my moving line. Once again, my long-term goal would have been for Mona to walk in line with her classmates on a consistent basis without causing disturbances.

Transitions are Mona's worst times of the day, with the last fifteen minutes being the most chaotic. My videotape captured her behavior and helped me to realize those final fifteen minutes were the images that stuck with me and not the norm of the day. By having Mona help with end of the day tasks, those chaotic minutes have almost completely subsided. In fact, I have found Mona to be quite capable of being a true help. Allowing a child who is demonstrating disruptive behaviors to help is not usually the first choice of any teacher. Yet, this strategy has proven to be successful with Mona.

Since Mona seems to respond best to the positive, I created a behavior journal for her. The behavior journal focuses on Mona's good behavior and efforts. I kept a second journal to record Mona's unacceptable behavior and saved it for discussions with Mona's grandparents, her guardians. I have come to believe that focusing on the individual incidences is not productive. It is the big picture, the fact that her behavior is continually unacceptable, that is significant. Documentation is important for you and her grandparents to be able to help Mona, but the positive journal has proven to be more successful as far as Mona is concerned. I allowed Mona to take her journal with her, and I hope you will find it useful in your efforts to help her. If you need any other information, or if I can be of assistance, please feel free to contact me at…

Sincerely,

Kathleen Pickard

I've taken a great deal of space above to duplicate Kathleen's entire letter because I learned so much from it and expect you will also. Here was another of those "toss away" children, one who is likely to continue her destructive behavior, build on her negative reputation, and get passed on and on and on. Here, in Kathleen, is another teacher who took a stand and figured out how to assist. When we take the time to focus on one child, we learn about all of them. There are Monas in all of our schools. They act out and know the dean better than they know their classmates. Or they're invisible, fading into the walls, growing smaller each year. Their hope is a teacher who reaches in and draws them out.

Some people who read the next story might focus on Michael's poor grammar, which would certainly earn him a fail on any standardized test. I urge you to read the content of what Michael is saying and realize how much he has gained in Genevieve Bodnar's class. All children don't learn at the same pace, or in the same way, in spite of our mandated pacing plans or one-size-fits-all curricula. One of the greatest challenges in teaching is to teach the individual child within a group setting. We cannot allow any of our students to get lost in the crowd.

Invisible

Genevieve Bodnar

He sat in the back of the room, when he was there; he usually missed at least one day a week. His name was Michael and he had no interest in school. It was obvious from his demeanor that he believed I had nothing to offer him and that he was only there because he had to be there. His sixth-grade year would be no different from any other. He was set to wait it out.

I didn't realize at first what was going on. With the onset of a new school year in my inner-city school, I was busy organizing the classroom, learning about the students, and planning for the year ahead. Little by little, I became aware of his pattern of absences, coupled with consistent inattention in class and incomplete work. In a crowded inner-city classroom it would be easy to miss him. He never disrupted the class. He was the perfect invisible student, which added to the problem.

I made a conscious effort to speak to him. Every day that he came, I welcomed him excitedly. I tried to engage him in conversation, which was usually received with a quiet smile, a brief response, and then polite silence. I decided that the only way I could possibly reach him was through the passion I felt for what I was teaching, the literature. I read to the class every day, *Lafcadio* by Shel Silverstein, *The Watsons Go to Birmingham—1963* by Christopher Paul Curtis, and *Holes* by Louis Sachar. We discussed the literature, reacting to the pictures, the words and ideas created in our minds, making connections to our own lives, and feeling the emotions of the characters as if they were members of our class. As the year progressed, students assumed more responsibility for reading on their own, although I continued to read to them daily. I used grant money to purchase books for students to keep. They each added three titles to their personal libraries. Since many students had never owned a book before, these books became treasured possessions. I didn't know how Michael felt, he never said, but his attendance improved and he began to turn in work.

Once a month students gave presentations based on the novels that they were now reading in small groups. The presentations were videotaped. Michael took a more active role in the preparation and delivery of the presentations but he was still quiet and reserved, speaking only when he absolutely had to.

In May each student had the choice of reading one of three novels: *Scorpions* by Walter Dean Myers, or *Forged by Fire* or *Tear of a Tiger*, both by Sharon Draper. They then participated in buddy journaling with seniors at the local high school who were reading the same books. Finally, the classes came together and students met their mystery pen pals to celebrate the buddy program.

At the end of the year I asked students to complete a survey and a teacher report card evaluating my performance. I asked them to write any final reflections on the back of the report card. This is what Michael wrote: "I think my attidud tord readin has changed a great deal every since I went to this class. Ive found my inner self. Ive found the poet within my. I uncoverd a side of me that I never knew I had. You Ms. Bodnar inspires the iner poet inside of me and ispires me to get my grades up and get rollin becuas theres not much time to improve. And don't tell knowbody this but befor I went to this class I never read ahole chapter book. But when I come to this class I did. I fergot what it was called." My invisible student was no longer transparent. This was just a beginning for Michael.

The future holds promise, but I worry about what will happen to Michael in the ensuing years. There are too many Michaels working alone in rows of desks and too few teachers to reach them.

Rereading the stories in final preparation for this collection, I am realizing anew how much of what we do as teachers, the truly important work, is about the relationships we build with our students. They are more than names and faces and numbers passing into, through, and beyond our classrooms. They're children, struggling with growing up, trying to yet shying away from accepting the consequences of their actions. Sometimes I wonder how long we should coddle them and how quickly we should expect them to stand on their own. I don't have an answer. While putting together this collection of classroom stories, and organizing them more or less equally into each of the five core propositions, it was always the students as individuals, more than anything else, that had the greatest pull and contributed to the largest chapter. At the end of the week, especially one that adds a few more gray hairs, you still have to love them.

His Words, His Way

Cheri J. Mann

Shane was nowhere near the brightest student or even the most attentive, yet he usually knew what was going on and always did whatever I asked. One day when I worked one-on-one with him after school to help him with his research paper, he gave me a glimpse into his world, expressing that the real Shane stays hidden because he's afraid no one will like him if they know who he really is. But I got to know the real Shane.

On the day before his graduation, he was revising his writing portfolio so that he could receive his diploma. We were in my room alone after school because he was banned from school during school hours due to having been caught smoking marijuana. As a result of that ban, he missed the senior picnic, the senior luncheon, and watching the senior video with friends he had known since kindergarten. I wondered, along with others, whether that would even have an effect on him and if the punishment fit the crime.

While I was reading over his work that afternoon, he rose and went to my whiteboard where he began: "Dear Seniors," Shane was a struggling writer. His spelling was so poor that sometimes even the spell check became speechless, providing no options to choose from. He took forever to write. I was surprised, then, when I saw him writing, and I sat in wonderment as he found his voice. For a half hour he crafted a note to his classmates that also included messages to me and to other teachers and coaches he'd had during his high school years. About halfway through I heard him sniffling and saw him wiping his eyes with the back of his hand. But he continued writing and ended up writing more than I'd ever seen him write in one sitting. He was crying when he finished, so I hugged him and we cried together. Shane had always been seen as a tough, macho man, rough-and-tumble football player, someone who wouldn't shed a tear if you cut his arm off. Yet here he was, drowning in his tears. With his head on my shoulder he said, "I wish I could be there." All I could do was whisper back, "So do I, so do I." Part of the punishment in this zero tolerance climate was not being able to attend his high school graduation ceremony. Not as a graduate. Not even as a spectator.

Shane had been in trouble before and accepted the consequences of his actions, usually, with ease. I no longer wondered whether the punishment affected him, yet I still had to hope that this time the con-sequences would change his life beyond one day, one week, or even one month.

As it turned out, Shane, in a sense, did attend graduation because I printed his words and had them waiting for his classmates when they reached their seats in the gymnasium. When we bowed our heads for prayer, they were able to read Shane's blessing for them. He spoke confidently through those words, wishing he could walk with them, but knowing he could not, and asking them to think of him as they accepted their diplomas and recalled the times they had spent together. He wished them well, called them his brothers and sisters, and ended his blessing with "Love, Shane."

The adults whom he mentioned received their own copies. His for-mer basketball coach didn't cry when he read that he'd taken Shane "from a boy to a man" and shown him "the love of a father," but I could tell he wanted to because he smiled and gave half a chuckle as if to choke back the tears. It seemed that Shane, a poor kid with a gift for rap, had a way with words after all.

I've seen Shane several times since then. I told him how I'd wanted to sneak him in the door at graduation and showed him this story while I was writing it. He always hugs me, asks how I'm doing, and gives me a big smile. I think he's doing okay, staying out of trouble at least, and trying to make something of himself. I guess that with a little guidance, he found his words and he may just find his way.

Fortunately, not all of our interactions with students are so serious; sometimes you just have to laugh at the kids and the way they express themselves. I had a student one year who insisted on wearing bright blue lipstick. I couldn't help it, but every time I looked up to ask a question or participate in a discussion, there would be her super enlarged blue lips smiling back at me. I couldn't help myself. Sometimes I'd lose it and just bust up laughing. One day after class I called her aside and admitted that even though I tried to accept all students as they came, the spiked hair, the grunge clothing draped with chains, and the blue lipstick, I just couldn't do it. I feared that the lipstick, more specifically my reaction to it, was hurting her academically. I called upon her for help. Shortly thereafter she stopped wearing the blue lipstick to class, whether because what I said had made an impact or because she had grown tired of it, I don't know, but at least it was gone. Getting rid of the lipstick was relatively easy, but other student behaviors prove more challenging and may carry on into adulthood.

There's a man, he must be about 40 by now, who attends the same summer concert series I do. During the concerts he sits on a low stool, the bottom of a cardboard box resting on a low portable table in front of him gathering the change people toss. In his left hand is a raggedy dog puppet, not too clean, not too realistic, but the same dog for at least the dozen years I've seen him there. The man sings away, manipulating the dog's mouth in mock imitation of a singer, only it's not very pretty. He's not a ventriloquist because he makes no effort to keep his own lips from moving. He's just a singer pretending the sounds are coming from his pet dog. He's become a fixture at the concert series and his box fills with coins and dollars after every performance. I've been watching him for years. I learned that he's a bookkeeper who also sings in his church choir, hopefully without the dog. He lives alone not far from the concert hall, and he performs elsewhere throughout the city. What I can't figure out is what's going on. Is his odd behavior an indication of a slightly unbalanced mental state or has he just figured out an approach that gets him what he wants—some attention and a box of money? I've often wondered how he was as a child, whether or not his behavior was unusual even then. Did his teacher notice anything odd? When I received Sharon Chaney's story, I wondered the same thing about her student and his dog. Would her intervention change the course of her student's life or would he someday take over the low stool and the cardboard box?

What Dog?

Sharon Chaney

Heading most lists of educational concerns, classroom management is a critical component for successful teaching. Parents demand it, politicians platformize it, administrators enforce it, and teachers seek magic formulas in order to achieve it; nevertheless, some students seem to sabotage even the most carefully crafted plans for classroom learning.

Such a student appeared in my college-bound class of juniors. Let's call him Kevin. Tall and handsome, Kevin was a favorite among his classmates. A particularly talented baseball player, he also attended all the basketball and football games to support his friends. He planned parties at his home and invited everyone. Because his blond hair fell casually over his bright eyes, he frequently flung his head to the right, freeing his vision for a moment. I was most concerned with neither his physical appearance nor his mounting popularity. Obviously, Kevin would be popular even without my help. My preliminary observation of Kevin's work in College Prep English III was his complete misunderstanding of—or disregard for—directions. Try as I might to surround him and his classmates with multiple written and oral sets of directions, Kevin just didn't pay attention to directions.

Clearly, a major reason for his inattention was the presence of an imaginary dog that he brought with him to class each day. Pretending to soothe the nonexistent pet, Kevin stroked the air in the imagined shape of the dog's head. Much to the delight of the other students, the dog "barked" and "moaned" during class at the most inopportune times. At first, I was almost as amused by this behavior as were his classmates. It did not occur to me that such behavior would continue, day after day. Nor did it seem appropriate to send Kevin to the office. "I can take care of this," I promised myself. "Besides, what can an administrator do to help with this situation?" I mused.

First, I had a talk with Kevin and his pet, suggesting that they must work together to understand and complete all of the assignments. Kevin agreed, and the dog yapped. Next, I gave split grades, one for Kevin and one for his pet, explaining that the two of them must share responsibility for their behavior and work. Kevin grinned, and the dog moaned. It was becoming clearer to me that Kevin cared most of all about providing entertainment for the other students in our class.

Acting on this possibility, I decided to strike boldly. I moved Kevin and his dog to a desk facing the front wall of the classroom. There they must stay until their behavior earned them a reward. With each half hour of exemplary behavior, both Kevin and dog could move backward, the width of one floor tile only, back into the class. Naturally, the reverse could also occur.

This procedure worked beautifully. Separated from his audience by the teacher, who was intercepting all attention, Kevin and his dog learned to coexist within a community of learners. Gradually, the dog stayed home, and Kevin relied on more mature, academic means of impressing others. Through it all, the other students were patient with both me and Kevin. At the outset, at least, they had understood his needs much better than I. As I worked toward a solution, other students became my allies in a consistent attempt at establishing and maintaining a learning environment. Kevin himself learned to concentrate, during class at least, on his considerable academic abilities. I learned a lesson, too: dealing directly with distracting behavior, however unusual, that students bring with them into the classroom can yield positive results. I never did figure out what the dog was all about or what happened to it. I was just relieved that Kevin came to class without his pet.

Great teachers welcome every student who enters the classroom and seek ways to help them achieve academically and socially. Some present challenges like Kevin and his dog, or my student with her blue lipstick, while others have much greater issues that require much more thoughtful responses. William Dean applied what he learned about multiple intelligences to help his students reach their potential. When his students have challenges that call for individualized teaching strategies, he doesn't attempt to figure out all of the answers himself. William asks his students about their learning, about what would help them the most, and then he listens to what they have to say. We all need to remember that students are not receptacles teachers throw knowledge into; they are partners in the classroom.

A Student's Road to Success

William Dean

When Amir, a special education student with a speech impediment, who had been homeschooled for three years, enrolled in my ninth-grade humanities class, I knew I needed to provide many activities and pathways for him and for the other students to succeed. Amir embodied all my students' need to have individual opportunities to show their critical and creative thinking skills.

In spite of working below grade level, Amir was highly motivated, participated in all classroom activities, and was ready to learn every day. He always completed his homework daily and was closely monitored by his supportive parents. Nevertheless, he required more time than did the other students to complete class assignments, and he definitely needed alternative reading assessments. Because he struggled with just completing his reading assignments and understanding them on a level with the rest of the class, I asked him how I could differentiate my instruction to meet his needs. He suggested that I require him to read half of what the others did because he would be able to keep up that way. He promised me that he would produce better work if he had sufficient time, and I gave it to him.

We had daily conferences to discuss the reading. He read excerpts or listened to entire chapters on tape. Whenever I assigned long-term exercises or projects or weekend activities, I provided choices from which Amir and the other students could select. Each student took two multiple intelligences self-inventories and engaged in other activities that enabled them to study their strengths and weaknesses as learners. Amir relished the opportunity to make choices: "I like the fact that I can choose what I want to do, and you let me change it when I need to." Like Amir, the other students took ownership of their learning by making good choices for assignment completion and project productivity. In fact, Amir and his classmates sometimes said, "I have a couple of ideas to add to our assignment list."

When it came time for Amir and the others to complete an end-of-the-unit project after reading *Parrot in the Oven: Mi Vida*, an autobiographical memoir, we reviewed a list of activities that connected to the eight multiple intelligences we'd studied throughout the year. Students selected projects aligned to areas in which they were strong. Amir completed a three-dimensional map of the character's neighborhood, along with an explanation of the design and impact of the character's neighborhood on his life. It was a joy to watch him stand before the class to present his project. His confidence minimized his speech problem. Other students experienced success as well. They displayed their visual and spatial strengths by designing a family crest, which represented the main character's traits, skills, and dreams. Several students created board games, a reading comprehension test on the book, and videos that depicted characters in scenes that reflected the book's themes.

I observed and documented my students' steady progress because I identified, nurtured, and supported their unique capabilities. I was elated by their consistent involvement in making choices that contributed to their success. After all, for me it was all about affirming that all students can learn. Amir proved that.

Secondary teachers often feel overwhelmed by the sheer number of students they see every day. When I worked in the corporate milieu, I never had to manage more than a dozen projects at a time, and usually many fewer than that. I never had more than a half dozen people who were directly responsible to me. In business there are layers of managers so no one directly takes charge of more than about 15 to 20 employees. Yet high school teachers in inner-city schools sometimes have a daily teaching load approaching 200 students. Teachers are amazing in their ability, in spite of the numbers, to see every child. We have to remember that sometimes our teaching is more effective when we focus, as Odessa Cleveland did, on one student and thereby learn how to assist all students.

Our Journey

Odessa Cleveland

At the beginning of the school year my students complete a questionnaire that guides me in reviewing and redesigning the course of study for a meaningful experience in English Language Arts. What changes will I make? How complex will the academic rigor be? How engaged will my students be while developing their language arts skills: listening, speaking, writing, reading, viewing, and publishing both print and nonprint media in a technological age?

When Rebecca stated, "I can't write good enough for your project," I knew if I assisted her through the writing process, if she collaborated with me and with her classmates, and if together we documented her progress, she would be engaged in academic rigor and accountable talk while improving her skills. Rebecca, a shy adolescent who had the looks of a beautiful rosebud, thought her doubts about herself would discourage me from working with her. Instead of being discouraged, I became more determined to help her succeed and meet the high standards I had for the class.

Rebecca listened attentively while I explained the objectives of the photo essay assignment. Students were to select a photo they had taken as the subject for an essay. Rebecca made notes on a Venn diagram that compared writing to photography. Together we reviewed her prewriting activities. I read drafts. We discussed her revisions in student conferences. She asked questions for clarity and made corrections as we talked about improving sentence structure, writing figures of speech, and punctuating correctly. I watched and kept anecdotal notes on her progress as she completed interim activities that helped her to improve her writing skills. She expressed her reasons for selecting a photo of her niece as the subject for the final essay. I continued reviewing and reflecting on her progress and group work; I encouraged her to revise her drafts yet one more time.

When Rebecca finished reading her final essay to the class I was tempted to remind her of her earlier doubts. Instead I just said, "Great job! Not only can you write, but the photo you took shows your potential as a serious photographer." Rebecca returned to her seat, sat down, and smiled shyly. She and her peers felt empowered. I felt empowered because the journey had challenged each of us. Although I've written about Rebecca, the journey involved all of my students. Rebecca's struggle caused me to reflect more on my professional practice than ever before. By closely examining one student's progress, I learned how students progress toward becoming effective writers.

We impact our students in ways we can't even predict. We hope the impact we make will be positive, as it was for Judith Chalmers' former student Lauren. We worry about those challenging students we never hear from or about once they leave our classrooms. There isn't a homeless person I see on our city's streets, or someone standing outside a hardware store waiting for a day's employment, or a young criminal I read about in the paper that I don't wonder if there was anything a teacher might have done or said that could have set this life in a more positive direction.

At least equal to any specific thing we might say or do, we are role models for our students. How we speak to one another, to our students, how we dress, handle ourselves, use language, how we react to other students, all of that combined behavior makes an impression on students. Teachers are held to a higher standard, because it matters. There's no room for us to act differently than we ask our students to act or to be less than we want our students to be. Like most teachers, we want to save the world, one child at a time. And although I found myself, while reading Judith Chalmers' story, thinking about Lauren's brother more than about Lauren, Judith's story is another reminder to spend some time basking in our successes.

You Just Never Know

Judith A. Chalmers

I have been teaching first grade at the same school since my husband retired from the military twelve years ago. It has been so nice to watch my first graders grow up and move on to middle school and high school and then return to say hello and let me know how they are doing. At the beginning of this year I had an experience that opened my eyes to the importance teachers can play in the lives of their students.

One day as I was eating lunch, the secretary paged me for a telephone call. When I answered the phone, a voice said, "Hi, Mrs. Chalmers. This is Lauren. Do you remember me?" I repeated the name to myself until I could see in my mind's eye a little blonde-haired girl. Of course I remembered her, but her family had moved away and I had not seen her in at least seven years. The family was living on the other side of Oklahoma. She said she was thinking about me and wanted to thank me for helping her to turn out to be a wonderful girl. She was a sophomore and doing well in school. She informed me that her parents had divorced. I had taught her younger brother and asked how he was doing. She replied that her parents had to go with him to court that very day and he would be going either into a state juvenile facility or to jail. I didn't know how to respond, so I stammered some platitudes. Before she said goodbye, she asked for my e-mail address.

At home that evening, I read her e-mail message. She wrote, "When I was in the first grade with you...you made a major impact on my life! And that was a great thing! You really inspired me to take my goals, set them, and put them to the highest that I could! And because of how well you worked with me, helped me and taught me, I was really thinking a lot about you today and how much I would love to get a great BIG hug from you! I want you to know you are the one that made me feel like I can be something and just go for it! And you know what, I did! And I still am."

As I thought about that year Lauren was in my class, I couldn't pick out anything special that I had done as a teacher. Lauren was a smart, quiet first grader who needed extra time and a little encouragement to finish her work. I had high expectations for her, as I do all my students.

Why had she called me? I realized the answer when I reread her last line— "Thank you for being there when I needed someone!" It was not her high test scores or her school success that made her seek me. With her life being so unsettled, she needed to go back to a simpler time and she remembered a teacher who gave her hugs and encouragement in first grade.

Over the months I spent collecting stories for this book and classifying them into each of the core propositions—a monumental task since the propositions are so interwoven and the complexities of our teaching traverse them all—I was struck anew by the personal and emotional domains that affect learning. These are the things we don't learn about in traditional teacher education programs. Knowing our students takes heart and soul. We can learn the craft of teaching, but the art comes from within.

In addition to preparing her lessons, Rosemary Fryer took the time to learn about her students' lives. That knowledge, at least as much as Rosemary's pedagogical skills and content knowledge, created the conditions for student Rebecca's success.

From Cocoon to Butterfly: Up Close and Personal

Rosemary Fryer

When Rebecca stood before an audience of 90 of her peers to state her opinion about violent television programming, my heart swelled with expectation, my throat went dry in anticipation. I wasn't certain that any words would come from Rebecca's lips, and if they did, would those words make sense? I knew Rebecca shook with fear, perhaps even terror as she faced her waiting audience. From behind the podium Rebecca spoke into a microphone, an instrument of intimidation, especially to one so shy.

Rebecca arrived at our school after moving into a shelter. Homeless for a few months, Rebecca and her mother had found temporary permanence, and Rebecca reenrolled in school, entering in the middle of the second trimester. Identified as a special education student, Rebecca at first didn't speak to anyone. Somewhere along the way Rebecca had decided that withdrawal and reticence would protect her from any connectedness, any friendships that could disappear at a moment's notice, given her tenuous home life. Besides, she had enrolled late, after the other students had already bonded. I'm sure Rebecca felt like an interloper, an outsider in a private world.

Since I consider my ability to establish knowledgeable and positive and enduring relationships with all my students as one of my strengths, I knew that getting to know Rebecca would present a considerable challenge. Until I could learn Rebecca's identity and make her a part of our class community, I would not be capable of engaging her in learning. All my students pervade the thoughts running through my mind daily, yet Rebecca's pale, sad face, flashed in and out of my brain's activity more and more often. Rebecca dominated my thinking. I carefully crafted a plan of action.

Each day I gave Rebecca a little more attention. I noticed her hair, her clothes, her jewelry or nail polish, any detail on which I could compliment her. One day Rebecca wore a royal purple skirt with a matching turtleneck shirt. She had applied makeup that brightened her face. Purple was her color, and I highlighted that fact in our first real conversation since she had entered our school. Progress, I thought, one small step toward a relationship.

Another element of my plan consisted of recruitment. I enlisted the help of some of my students to reduce Rebecca's anxiety about her environment and befriend her without making any demands. Nikki, Lisa, and Dustin began to include Rebecca in the routine work of class. Day by day, Rebecca became a bit more comfortable in social exchanges. Soon the final exam for the trimester loomed before us—a formal debate, an exhibition of verbal expertise.

I knew Rebecca could handle the written requirement of this final project, for my teammates and I had constructed a step-by-step structure that made the writing piece achievable for all of our students. Yet the speaking part presented a problem, not only for Rebecca but also for all the timid students on our team. Not wanting to single out Rebecca as the shyest student, or even hint that she may not be capable of being in front of an audience, I taught a mini-lesson on "tips for lips" to dispel some of the scariness that public speaking instills in the hearts of most people. I asked Rebecca how I could help her; her teammates asked too. At her suggestion, they rehearsed; they speculated about the opposition's arguments; they prepared responses to every argument they thought might come up. In every instance they reached out to Rebecca, as I did, affirming the value of her efforts and encouraging her participation.

The day arrived for the games to begin. Rebecca dressed for success in her purple skirt and matching turtleneck. She looked super! When I called for the issue, a nervous but ready team of 10th graders took their places at opposite tables. The signal was given; the debate began. Soon enough, the time of reckoning loomed. I held my breath. Rebecca went to the podium, and to my delight, she presented her piece in a clear voice, while making eye contact with her audience. After the teams had finished, the audience could question either side for further insight into the issue. Rebecca fielded questions well. Wow! How cool was that! A hint of tears crept into the corners of my eyes. Rebecca's victory reminded me, in my mind and in my heart, that teaching reaches beyond instruction; teaching is up close and personal.

We teach the Rebeccas who come into our lives through the classroom door, and we also learn from them. We teach them the curriculum, Math and Science, Literature and Art, and we learn courage through their lives and through their resiliency. Every day they come to our classrooms, from homeless shelters, from mountaintop estates, from city streets and country roads. They come carrying the myriad lessons of their lives. There are students who have touched me so deeply I thought I was filled to overflowing and had no more room for anyone else, but still they come, and there's always room. Students, like my own children, help to keep me human and focused on what is important. When I was in the business and corporate community, we measured success by the size of our offices, the newness of our leased cars, and the toys we accumulated. In teaching, it's not about who has the most toys, it's about touching lives and being touched. I'm richer now than I have ever been.

The Pelican Way

Kathryn Gemmer

I first met her when I was a guest on a hike with the Outdoor Club. The biology teacher that I was to replace the following year had invited me along to meet some of the kids that I would be sponsoring in the future, and she was there, talking incessantly in the manner of sophomores. Straight blonde hair, crystal blue eyes, and a swaggering stride that was at ease in the woods are imprinted in my memory. I remember her that day in particular because she lingered about halfway through the hike to ask me about the trees that had been gnawed on by the beavers. Did I think we would see one? She loved biology. She loved the outdoors.

For the next several years she became a part of my life. At the beach her laughter permeated the class because of her amazement at the pelicans and the awkward way they dove. Her entire field assignment was about pelicans. "Pelicans are cool," she'd say. And as I read her field notes, I had no choice but to agree. Megan was that way. Other students loved eagles and osprey. She loved the pelicans, the underdogs. They were not pretty or lovable, fighting their way from the threat of extinction in a quiet, determined way. "The Pelican Way," she called it, and then laughed.

I hiked with Megan in drenching rains, pressed her to push herself in advanced exams, and watched her scrap on the basketball court as if the game were a match of spunkiness instead of athletics. In all of these instances her laughter would give way to a restless stare; her crystal eyes full of a quiet determination.

I remember her freshman year in college. I received an e-mail from her. She wanted me to come and watch her presentation for an Environmental Science class for which she had diligently prepared. That same resolute stare, so familiar, met me that day at the door. She wanted to go to a bigger university. She was impatient and the students were not as serious about important issues as she felt they needed to be. As if to press her point, her presentation was brilliant. She had spent a lot of time measuring light pollution and recording the impact of its effects. I was proud of her. She was one of "my kids."

Over the months there were more visits and more e-mails. She attended a larger university and tackled a serious biology curriculum. But along the way came rounds of chemotherapy and myriad doctor visits. The straight blonde hair came out lock by lock. The incessant chattering was replaced with mature and thoughtful conversation. Her swaggering stride faltered. However, one thing remained. That determined stare, those impatient blue eyes, so familiar to me. And I was proud of her. She was one of "my kids."

Megan exemplifies the two-way street that is the teaching profession. She gave to me the beauty of pelicans. She taught me not only lessons in biology, but lessons in life. I teach because of this intangible. I teach because of "my kids."

When I came to the classroom after years in the business community, I wasn't prepared, in spite of my newly acquired credential and graduate classes, for all I would encounter. Students were not all the perfect academics waiting to be filled with the knowledge I had to impart to them. Their lives weren't something out of *Father Knows Best* and they certainly weren't all modeled after *The Brady Bunch*. Nevertheless, we can't afford to throw away a single one. Nor can we label them and shove them aside. And we can't allow them to continue destructive behavior either. Often the students we struggle with the most leave the deepest marks.

First Comes Love

Wendy Hacke

I first met Aaron when he was 6 years old and I was a behavior specialist running a collaborative program for the seriously emotionally disturbed (SED) students in our school district. I was often used as a resource for students who were acting out in unsafe ways. Aaron was a referral. By the time I met him, he had already been indirectly responsible for four broken arms and two broken noses. It was the principal's hope that through observation and assessment by the district psychologist and me Aaron would be placed in a SED program and would be out of his school, and someone else's problem.

As part of information gathering I met with Aaron's former first-grade teacher. She told me that after meeting Aaron she decided he belonged in Special Education classes and therefore spent no time at all to assist him academically. She made this decision in the belief that if she could demonstrate Aaron wasn't progressing academically, then he would get the help he really needed in a Special Education setting. She meant well, but was all wrong. In an interview Aaron's parents indicated they wanted to help with his behavior management, but the principal said the parents had been neither supportive nor accessible in the past. There was animosity on both sides even before I arrived.

After a thorough assessment the district psychologist and I concluded that Aaron was not a Special Education candidate, what he needed was play therapy to help him learn to play appropriately on the playground, where all the former incidents occurred. We also believed he was experiencing heightened frustration because he lacked the academic support he craved. We recommended a classroom setting and required a behavior contract. We would provide lots of positive reinforcement. The principal disagreed with our findings and placed Aaron in a self-contained day class.

When the new school year began, Aaron was in a special day class and I was teaching a first and second grade combination. When Aaron's new teacher told me he was academically head and shoulders above the other students we decided he would come to my room every day for math. My students were not thrilled, they all knew Aaron and his unsocial behavior on the playground, but over time we worked through how important it is to accept all children. We used a behavior management contract and Aaron thrived, so much so that I often forgot to return him to his Special Education class after the math hour concluded.

I called Aaron's parents regularly, focusing on Aaron's positive behavior. Even when they asked, "What did Aaron do wrong today?" I countered with his positive actions. I wanted to build a trusting relationship with them so if there were a repeat incident we could work on solving it as partners, not adversaries. Before too long there was a playground incident when Aaron pushed a classmate who wouldn't allow him to join a football game. The parents and I came together determined we would continue to reinforce Aaron's positive behavior while at the same time letting him know that the negative behavior was not acceptable and wouldn't be tolerated. At home, his parents praised the positive and downplayed the negative.

By December, Aaron's positive behavior improved significantly and he was removed from Special Ed classes and returned to a general education classroom—mine. Aaron's success presented itself in multiple ways. His classmates began seeking him out for help in math, his strongest subject. He became a cross-age tutor for the first graders and his reading skills jumped. Best of all, Aaron learned to get along well with his classmates, even when they didn't do what he wanted; incidents of aggressive behavior dwindled, but didn't disappear.

A few years later, after Aaron and I had each moved to other schools, I learned through a colleague that Aaron's behavior was regressing. His parents and I had worked too hard to keep him out of Special Ed classes for me to allow this to pass unnoticed. I sent Aaron a letter reminding him of all he'd accomplished, of how hard he had worked to control his behavior, and how important it was that he not slip back. Our bond must still have been strong because his teacher reported that Aaron smiled when he received my note. She also told me that after the letter he settled down and she had no other troubles with him. The bonds I develop with my students, especially with the students whose needs are greatest, leave an indelible mark on me and apparently on them also.

We want our students to soar, to leave our classrooms prepared for future success, ready to realize their dreams. Although occasionally we do light that fire under our students and really propel them far beyond what they expected, it usually doesn't happen that way. Foster Walsh's story is powerful in that it reminds us that success is often measured in inches. We need to accept that growth even in inches, where there was none before, is still success.

Success: Measured in Inches, Not Feet

Foster Walsh

Pat didn't want a D in 10th-grade English, so he asked what he could do to raise his grade. I told him to take the class more seriously and to complete all of his assignments on time—a response I have given to Pat before. Pat assured me that his attitude and work ethic would improve. But again, nothing new happened. In spite of his desire for a higher grade, Pat didn't like English and his writing efforts reflected this level of interest. I asked Pat on several occasions to select a writing topic that interested him, still without much success. Pat, like some of my students, frustrated and confused me. I alternated between moving toward Pat, peppering him with possible writing topics, and just giving up. I desperately wanted to reach him because he had the ability to do well. But he was sarcastic and overly negative, which made him difficult to reach. On his other side he had the tenderness of a teddy bear once you deflected his cutting remarks.

My initial understanding of Pat's literacy skills and his attitudes toward literacy came from a reading–writing survey all students completed during the first week of school. From his comments it was clear that Pat hated writing, disliked English, and barely tolerated school. As was my custom, I began the writing unit by using the KWL strategy, asking my students two initial questions: (1) What do you know about writing and (2) what do you want to know about writing? Pat responded with his normal, passive-aggressive humor saying, "I know about diagramming sentences" and "I want to know when we will be finished with this writing stuff." Pat used his well-honed wit to mask his insecurity and to irritate me. It almost worked. Probing further, I asked students what they liked and disliked about writing. With a smirk, Pat said, "I like finishing and I dislike starting." He responded with a terse, but empathic "NO!" when asked if he wanted to improve his writing.

In the midst of this interplay of pursuing teacher and unmotivated student, I discovered two things that Pat liked to do. He liked to express his opinion and he liked to play football—his 5'11," 250-lb. frame produced lots of gridiron accomplishments. I urged Pat to write a letter to the College Bowl Series President, expressing his strongly held opinion about the college selection process.

Pat's paper, titled "Letter to John Doe," followed the letter of complaint structure, but lacked attention to detail and contained multiple errors in all the traits of quality writing. He obviously did not take the process of constructing his paper seriously. Despite suggestions for improvements, Pat merely copied his initial draft for the final submission. How could I reach Pat? Giving up looked like a good option, especially after a colleague, having a rough day himself, suggested, "Let him hang himself."

My years of experience have taught me that the students who are the most unlovable are the ones that most need love—a nice statement, but did it apply to Pat? The bottom line was I didn't want to give up on Pat or on any of my students. I chose to persevere, and I am glad I did.

Before Pat's second paper I scheduled an early morning appointment with him. I brought donuts and whipped cream for hot chocolate and proceeded to get to know Pat. I tried to find out what made him tick, what he did with his free time, what his favorite TV shows were, and who were his best friends. We talked about everything but English. That mini breakfast was the first in a series of Friday morning meetings spent listening to an insecure adolescent talking about his life.

Pat's second paper was more mediocre work, but there were several notable differences. Pat secured two peer edits, one more than on his first paper. He actually made several minor revisions to improve his text. Pat's final product had not dramatically improved, but it was better, and he was proud of it. Pat asked twice as many questions and made twice as many textual changes. He believed he had produced quality work, and for Pat, he had.

Pat taught me that school successes are measured in inches, not feet. I was reminded again that relationship can achieve what no amount of content knowledge or aversive control can. I rediscovered that moving toward my students is scary and exciting and profoundly rewarding. At our next early morning conversation, Pat thanked me for the donuts and said, "Mr. Walsh, you are an OK English teacher." We'd begun; inches, not feet.

There are all manner of reasons why students act out, many the result of events in their lives outside of school. Regardless of the cause, we see a lot of inappropriate behavior. Secondary students get sent to the dean or suspended. Elementary students get time-outs. For some, it's that special teacher who sees beyond the negative behavior to the child beneath. You've already read several stories of teachers' reaching beyond the behavior in order to get to the student. In order to be an effective teacher, to develop a classroom of learners, you must provide an emotionally safe environment. Here's another story about the student behind the behavior.

Finding Miguel

Damien Riley

During my second year of teaching fifth grade, I met Miguel, and years later he's still with me. Miguel was a smart fifth grader, but a tantrum thrower on the playground. By midyear his social-behavioral problems were limiting his ability to take part in many of our cooperative learning activities. As a result, he was falling behind academically. I learned in an SST (student support team, parent–administrator–teacher) conference that he had been abandoned by his mother at age 3 and thereafter lived with his grandmother who was sickly and scarcely able to take care of herself. Because there wasn't much assistance possible from the home, I decided I needed to give Miguel the extra attention he needed.

When Miguel felt someone was leaving him out or ignoring him in any way, he'd sob. When the person or group continued to ignore him, he'd yell profanities at them. On a few occasions, I found him rolling on the floor kicking and screaming because he was so angry. Miguel was not a typical kid, and he needed much more time and energy than I could possibly allocate to him in a class of 35, in spite of my good intentions. By midyear, he had lost his zest for school, but I hadn't.

I decided I would try to inspire him through his interests. Each time I spoke with Miguel I listened for signs of his favorite things. I wanted to motivate him to take part in the classroom and thought connecting to something he already liked might help. Alas, he seemed to have no interests other than "N64" and watching TV. I was ready to abandon my plan. I despaired of finding any interests I could use as a bridge to help Miguel. But one day just after dismissal, that all changed.

After the students had received their dismissal high-fives, I returned to the class computer and began typing notes into my journal. I heard Miguel behind me rustling his backpack and assumed he was on his way out. After a few minutes, however, I realized he was fascinated watching me type. On a whim I gave him a floppy disk and told him, if he wanted to, he could stay in at recess each day and write in a journal he could open on the computer. I told him I would save his entries on the special disk and keep it for him.

By the end of the year, Miguel had almost written an autobiography. He found something he liked to do, and it improved his attitude knowing each day he would have the opportunity to do it. To my delight, his grades came back up, and his social skills improved. After I gave him a high-five the last day of school, I presented him with the full disk he had gradually created. I drew a happy face on it in a red sharpie and wrote, "Never underestimate yourself." He blushed as he accepted his project on the disk and avoided eye contact. Nevertheless, a big ear-to-ear grin said volumes about what the disk meant to him.

I learned from Miguel that finding those blossoming interests and curiosities of students can be the secret weapon against apathy and anger. I will always remember Miguel fondly as a result of that lesson. I hope, even now, he is still finding new and wonderful things to be interested in.

Sometimes in the rush to get through the curriculum, preparing students for seemingly endless rounds of testing, and balancing lesson planning with assessment, we lose sight of the students. Each comes to us as a precious individual, with unique gifts. And each child, sometimes overtly, sometimes not, offers us the gift of self, even when it's disguised as a cookie.

A Gift of Cookies

Ann Matthys Smalley

The children who enter my kindergarten classroom are moving from the world of family and home to the world of formal public education. It is essential to their future school lives that in kindergarten we establish a bond of trust with each of them. Trust is indispensable for developing an environment conducive to risk taking, a necessary ingredient of learning to flourish. In a safe environment, mistakes become opportunities to learn. In our community of learners, I constantly learn from and with my students, and as an intent kid-watcher, I seek to find each student's place on the learning continuum. When high expectations are coupled with a focus on what a student knows, one can use a student's interests and unique learning styles to open pathways to new understandings.

Timothy, a thin, quick-moving 6-year-old, often arrived at school without backpack or supplies. From the very beginning of the school year, Timothy took snacks from classmates' backpacks. He ate discarded lunch leftovers others deemed unfit for consumption. I checked with his parent who assured me he ate plenty at home. I checked with the school cafeteria who confirmed that he cleaned his plate during school breakfast and lunch. I didn't understand why Timothy continued to take his classmates' snacks.

Over time, I tried a number of strategies to remedy the situation. First we talked, then I threatened, I even brought a supply of cereal he could snack on in class. No matter what, Timothy still helped himself to others' treats. Then I tried giving him what he wanted, the power over his classmates' snacks. Instead of taking snacks from his classmates, Timothy would now be responsible for giving out snacks to them. As a result, I hoped he would no longer feel the need to sneak through belongings to find tempting morsels that he could quickly devour. Each morning, I collected student snacks and put them in a box high on a shelf until it was time for Timothy to distribute them. When snack time arrived, Timothy stepped up to the box, surveyed the contents, announced each treat, and waited for the rightful owner to claim the food. This proved to be a most effective management tool. In the eyes of his classmates, Timothy's dignity was restored and his status rose as he daily carried out his job of snack distributor.

One morning in December, shortly before our holiday break, Timothy witnessed a little girl excitedly skipping into the room. She handed me a gift box of candy. Timothy watched as I opened the box and exclaimed over the chocolates. Then he disappeared for a moment and returned with his hands hidden behind his back. Hesitantly, he approached my desk, bringing forth a ball of crumpled newspapers which he offered to me. "Here Ms. Smalley, I have a gift for you." With genuine surprise I replied, "Oh, Timothy, is this really for me?" and I held out my hands to accept his gift. When I unfolded the smudged newsprint, I discovered four chocolate cookies, a rare snack from

Timothy's home. My eyes filled with tears as I gazed upon a present only Timothy could give me. "Oh, Timothy, how did you know I love cookies so much? I am just a big cookie monster. This is one of the best presents I have ever received!" Timothy beamed a gap-toothed grin at me and for the rest of the day he seemed to walk in glory. Timothy had gone from stealing treats to sharing them, an important social skill he would need if he was to be successful in school and beyond. His gift from the heart was a gift to my heart and a reminder that we teach children first, not curriculum. Timothy had gone from being a child shunned by his classmates to being an important contributing member of our classroom learning community. We teach because touching a child's life is the most rewarding work in the world.

Early in my teaching career I read a story about a student that continues to reverberate with me. The story told about a young student, maybe 10 years old, who came to school every day but didn't talk to anyone. He sat quietly in his seat, did very mediocre work then went home at the end of the day. Because he wasn't disruptive, the teacher just let him sit. One day on the way home from school he just fell out of the bus and died. The story is supposed to be true, but whether it is or not doesn't really matter. The point here is that we can't allow students to be invisible.

I currently consult in a large urban high school that has more than 5,000 students on three different tracks spread throughout the year. They are working hard on forming smaller learning communities in order to mitigate the negative aspects of this massive establishment. The principal and his faculty are attentive to students' needs, but ensuring that students individually get the time and care, academically, socially, and in career advisement, they need is a monumental chore. I don't know how all of their efforts will play out, although I applaud them loudly for their labor. What I do know and have felt from the beginning is that no child within my care will be invisible. If each teacher makes that commitment, then there won't be any children left to fend for themselves.

REFLECTION

To test your own beliefs about student learning, try this simple reflection:

Say—Mean—Matter

Instructions

1. What do you say about your students? List 10 words or phrases that come to mind when you think or talk to others about your students.

2. What does what you say mean? Read your list. What do these words and phrases imply about what you believe about your students?

3. Why does what you say and mean about your students' learning matter so much? How does your belief about your students affect your teaching? The work you assign? Your expectations for them? Your expectations for yourself as a teacher?

RESOURCES

Our students are each unique. If you want to learn more about working with individual students while you work in your classrooms, here are some resources for you.

If you have time for only one book, read the following:
Levine, M. (2002). *A mind at a time: America's top learning expert shows how every child can succeed.* New York: Simon & Schuster.

If you have more time, select one or more of the following:
Finn, P. J. (1999). *Literacy with an attitude: Educating working-class children in their own self-interest.* Albany: State University of New York Press.
Gardner, H. (1993). *Multiple intelligences: The theory in practice.* New York: Basic Books.
Gregory, G. H., & Chapman, C. (2002). *Differentiated instructional strategies: One size doesn't fit all.* Thousand Oaks, CA: Corwin Press.

Scheidecker, D., & Freeman, W. (1999). *Bringing out the best in students: How legendary teachers motivate kids.* Thousand Oaks, CA: Corwin Press.

REFERENCES

Kadyszewski, H. (2003, March 4). Serious senioritis?: Fewer students say courses are meaningful. *Christian Science Monitor.*

Mack-Kirschner, A. (2003). *The teacher's guide to National Board Certification: Unpacking the standards.* Portsmouth, NH: Heinemann.

Marzano, R. J. (2003). *What works in schools: Translating research into action.* Alexandria, VA: Association for Supervision and Curriculum Development.

Teachers Know the Subjects They Teach and How to Teach Those Subjects to Students

When I decided to become a teacher there was never any doubt that I would teach high school English language arts. Step into my living room and you'll see thousands of volumes alphabetized in 30 feet of book shelves. When I talk about books, or bring books to class to entice students to read them, I'm excited and passionate. It's evident to my students that I love to read. I obtained a supplemental certificate in literacy so I'd know how to teach reading and writing so students can learn. I continuously add new strategies to my repertoire or improve those I already use so I can reach even my struggling readers. But although I think I have a good handle on which strategy to use and when, I struggle with which pieces of literature to teach for which students. I always consider what lessons or ideas will come from this piece of reading and then try to make the right choice given the very real constraints of time, what's available, the district mandates. . . . I want students to love reading, to read to learn, to be entertained, to be inspired, and more. Because we are important role models, our attitudes about what we teach are often what remain with students long after the factoids have been forgotten. As you read on you'll agree that Kelly Campbell-Busby's students will be art connoisseurs throughout their lives.

Some years ago I read an article by futurist Peter Schwartz (1996). In it he predicted that by the year 2020 information would double every 73 days. Since then I've been asking the teachers I work with, what in their subject is important for students to know and be able to do. There's a lot of head scratching involved in trying to come up with the answers, and just when you do there's a new discovery and we have to rethink what we're teaching. While accomplished teachers know the facts, the discreet bits of information, they also have a clear understanding of the big ideas, the essential understandings students need as foundations for future learning. We are continually juggling our content and its relevance to the rest of the world. National Board Certified Teacher Kathleen Blake, an art teacher, knows what's most important for her students to learn and be able to do, and she expresses her teaching philosophy well:

I want my classroom to reflect an atmosphere that promotes lifelong learners. I teach students that anyone can develop technique and skill, but great work comes from their attitude, their sincerity, and the heart and soul they put into their work. It is the heart and soul that creates leaders, makes better workers, and fosters conscientious community membership.

Although lesson planning takes up a great deal of our classroom time, there are always occasions when we have to let go of the lesson plan and go with the teachable moments. The stories in this chapter are all about teaching and learning—but that's the subject of the whole book, isn't it? Just another reminder that even when we try to break our content apart into teachable pieces, every piece connects to every other. There's the metaphor that says that even a butterfly's fluttering wings have enough power to create a tidal wave and thus change the world. For me this is a reminder that we teach students, not curricula, and it is our students who will change the world. Kathleen Blake knows this very well. She put her objectives aside and made room for Scott to express what he saw.

Rembrandt Comes in All Sizes

Kathleen A. Blake

I am a visual arts teacher. My students learn to see better in my class-room where perception is taught as intelligence. While there is much information that I teach students and want them to take in, it is equally important for me to teach them how to be reflective and how to draw from within to express themselves in their work.

Scott, a student I had several years ago, had a unique perspective of himself and his world. He came through my doorway almost every day bearing a grin from ear to ear, wearing a plaid flannel shirt, and carrying a twinkle in his eyes. He was full of life and energy, accented by his wild, strawberry blond hair. At the time, we were working on observation drawing. The ultimate goal was to achieve a resemblance to the objects that you saw. The first time I looked at Scott's drawing, I saw several different angles or perspectives of the objects we were copying; they appeared to be rendered in a style similar to cubism and looked quite primitive. Working from observation was difficult for Scott and his work looked different from the other students' who tried to recreate what they saw.

Although he tried realism, when Scott selected a piece of charcoal and began to draw, the abstract, expressive end result was still primi-tive in nature. Nevertheless, there existed a special quality in Scott's art. He captured boldness of expression and his work came alive with heart and soul. Scott and I discussed his art and he began to gain self-confidence. He knew that his work was different from the other students' but my words encouraged him, keeping him focused on the pure expression of the process of making art rather than on the end product.

When it came time for the Regional Scholastic Art Competition, I encouraged Scott to enter his art portfolio. He had many doubts and I reminded him that it was not about winning, it was about what he would learn in the process of preparing his work and entering the competition. He entered his portfolio. We were both disappointed that not one piece was selected for the regional exhibit. It just so happened, though, that the regional program director decided to forward all the portfolio entries to New York for national judging, whether or not they had won at the regional competition. He included Scott's slides in that shipment. Months later, we received a call from the awards committee. Scott's work was chosen as one of the top five portfolios in the nation. Scott was overjoyed, surprised, and humbled by the news. He traveled to Washington to accept his award at the Library of Congress.

When students enter my classroom, they soon understand that I believe they can succeed and that I will do everything I can to assist their learning. As the trust level grows, so does my relationship with each student and theirs with one another. The rapport that we establish becomes the backbone of all the discoveries, experiences, and knowledge I strive to give them. There is love and caring relationships in all accomplished teachers' classrooms. I believed in Scott, and he learned to believe in himself.

Our students spend more time watching TV and movies than they do in class. Consequently they believe the stereotypes the movies portray: scientists, like Eddie Murphy's *The Nutty Professor* (1996), are weird; mathematicians, like the one Russell Crowe portrayed in *A Beautiful Mind* (2001), hallucinate. The negative impressions students bring to the classroom sometimes present barriers to learning. Biology teacher John Dorroh discovered that uncovering the scientist within each student is a powerful strategy to break down the walls and encourage students to pursue math and science.

Collect, Select, and Reflect

John Dorroh

For most of my 27 years of teaching high school science, I have noticed at the beginning of each new school year that, for the most part, students have a negative connotation of the word *scientist*. Furthermore, when I tell them during the first day of class that each of them is a budding scientist, they look at me with bewildered expressions, often challenging me with arms folded across chests, claiming, "No way am I a scientist! I'm not a nerd." I go on to assure them that I am *certain* that they are scientists and that I will catch them in the act at least 10 times during the school year behaving, thinking, or writing like a scientist; they are just as determined to prove me wrong.

One of their first assignments is to write a rough draft for a composition titled "How I See Myself as a Scientist." The vast majority of the students extend the notion in this paper that they *do not* see themselves as scientists, citing evidence such as "scientists don't have personal lives," "scientists love to live inside a lab and never see the light of day," "scientists are weird nerds who have wild hair and smoking test tubes full of dangerous acids," and so forth. Only a few remember and admit that finding a lost set of keys by retracing their steps or finding out through personal interviews who started that nasty rumor about their best friend is a scientific behavior.

All students are required to maintain portfolios of their evaluated work. We keep the portfolios in boxes in the room. Once a month each student selects one "best" piece from his or her folder for reflection. "What element(s) of this selection show(s) me acting, thinking, or writing like a scientist? Why did I select it? If this piece is a springboard for a subsequent project, what would that project be? How could this piece have been improved?" After the piece has been analyzed and shared with a partner, the students place it in their portfolios, which are decorated with photos taken in the lab or in class. As the months pass, the folders become more personalized and begin to show how the students are reflecting "scientist behavior."

By early spring our class motto for portfolios becomes "Collect, select, and reflect." By May each student has 10 pieces in his or her folder, each piece contributing to the total picture of that student as a blossoming scientist. On selection days a unique portfolio culture replaces that of a day spent in small groups, in the lab, or in guided instruction. The language that the students use is different from a normal day, as is the overall atmosphere. The pace is slower and more deliberate. To an outsider, it might look more like an art class in session.

At the end of the school year students have in their possession a collection of their best work. Individual preferences are evident as well as growth over time. Students are proud of their portfolios. When asked, "Okay, do you now see yourself as a scientist?" most respond with a hint of a smile, "Well, maybe just a little."

Incorporating portfolios in my high school biology classes over the past 12 years has helped to break down the negative stereotype of scientists as nerds, as Hollywood often casts them. And when you ask me, "Have you helped your students to change their minds about being scientists?" with a hint of a smile, I respond, "Well, maybe just a little."

Although my initial reasons for creating this collection of classroom stories was not to provide lesson plans that could be duplicated, the more I read them the more I find myself pulling ideas for the work I do with classroom teachers. I learn about strategies that work by seeing the students through the story. Reading the stories increases my advocacy as well. I hope that everyone involved with determining budget allocations reads Kathleen's story above and Kelly's story below before they decide to cut the arts from education.

Elementary Artist Studies

Kelly Campbell-Busby

Why is it the things you think have nothing in common come together in ways that make so much sense you wonder why you didn't think of them sooner? Well, that is exactly what happened to me while preparing one of the portfolio entries for the Early to Middle Childhood Art certificate. I had participated in a 2-week reading–writing initiative our state offered the summer prior to starting my National Boards. Although I teach elementary art and do not usually teach reading and writing, I wanted to apply some of my newly acquired language arts knowledge to my class, but had not developed an avenue for it.

While preparing the National Board portfolio I questioned what I was teaching, why I was teaching what I taught, and if my students were really retaining any of the pertinent information I felt they should know about art and artists. Two totally separate curricula, or they seemed to be at the time, came together when I became frustrated with my original plan for the Portrait-Over-Time portfolio, so with less than 2 months left before school ended and my box was due I decided to change everything. Second grade was about to begin a unit on Vincent van Gogh, so I decided to use it for my entry. Crazy, I know, but working under pressure made me put all my creative teaching energy to the test. I scrambled to retrieve all the reading and writing information from the summer's workshops, gathered all the van Gogh information I could get my hands on, and created what has become known as *Artist Studies.*

For 8 weeks students were assessed on their knowledge of van Gogh using a graphic organizer called a KWL (K stands for what they think they know about a subject, W for what they want to know, and L for what they have learned). Parents helped create study folders that included the KWL, puzzles, texture studies, maps, and vocabulary lists. I also purchased six copies of the book *Getting to Know the World's Greatest Artists: Vincent van Gogh* by Mike Venezia. The second grade, all 80+ students, shared the books by reading them with a parent and then passing them along to another student. They answered questions about the reading, participated in class discussions, watched videos on van Gogh, and created art.

The second graders created sunflower drawings and sculptures, self-portraits, and impasto and torn paper landscapes. The study focused on the art elements of texture, color, line, and shape. The students and I enjoyed taking extra time during each class to discuss van Gogh's life and his artwork. Toward the end of the unit classes participated in the *L* part of the KWL to discuss what they had learned. It was not until much later that I realized how successful this in-depth study had been. During a class the following year we were playing an art version of To Tell the Truth, when I about fell out of my chair! Three students held prints of famous artworks and the class asked yes or no questions to determine who the famous artist was. When it came time to determine the *real van Gogh* the students asked probing questions they would have never asked had they not studied van Gogh in depth the year before. These were third graders discussing van Gogh's life and style.

Once I realized the impact of the in-depth study, I adapted the concept for the other grade levels. All grades, K–5, now participate in at least one Artist Study per year. Kindergarten studies Lois Ehlert with art projects based on her books, and they write critiques about their favorite pieces. First graders study Henri Matisse, creating drawings and collages, as well as having books read to them by their book buddies and myself. Third-grade students study Pablo Picasso through book shares and critiques and art projects based on his different styles.

Fourth grade studies famous women artists and participates in article and book shares and art projects imitating each woman's style. The fifth graders study famous sculptors with art projects and a research paper or gallery presentation.

The irony that Artist Studies ever came together amuses me now, but it was less than comical a few years ago. The success I have witnessed with my students makes all those tears and stressful moments worthwhile. The proof of studying topics in depth has me questioning every lesson and thinking about how it will be useful to my students once they leave elementary school. Those more "frills"-type lessons I once taught have been replaced with meaningful, retainable, and more exciting ones. My experience with National Board certification has, without a doubt, made me a better teacher. And as for my students, it has made them more knowledgeable lifelong learners whose lives will forever include art.

Teachers are always making choices about what is important to teach and about how to teach it. Language Arts teachers attempt to expose their students to a wide variety of literature. When the mandated curriculum is packed, we sometimes have to sneak in the pieces we're most drawn to. We keep our fingers crossed that we're making the right choices and that the book or idea will open a student's mind, engage the imagination, and allow the learning to happen. We're always juggling coverage and depth and trying to find the right balance. For Pamela Beery's student, Langston Hughes and the in-depth, nonconventional way Pam taught his poetry brought Eric to the front of the bus.

Not Just Another Field Trip

Pamela Beery

One evening, I was on a bus taking a group of students to see a production of *Anne Frank*. Bus trips are my least favorite part of teaching, so I was dreading the choruses of "100 Bottles of Beer on the Wall" and the motion sickness that I always get. I was amazed when from the back of the bus I heard Eric, a student who had arrived in my sixth-grade class reading at a third-grade level, begin to perform Langston Hughes' "African Dance." For the weeks before the trip, we were working on performing the poem in class. We took the rhythms of the poem and built rhythmic ostinatos, which we added to the performance on African instruments. Some of the students added a dance that included students portraying the fire and "the night veiled girl." It was a lesson that I used when I taught general music classes as a way to include nonsingers, or boys whose voices were changing, in our performances. I had decided to incorporate it in the Language Arts classroom simply because kids enjoyed it. Within minutes, my students taught the whole bus the poem and the rhythms. Students performed the poem by stomping, clapping, and pounding rhythms on the backs of the seats for almost an hour. It was a bus ride I'll never forget. That year Eric's reading level improved nearly two grades and he received an award for community involvement.

Although I had studied literature for years, I learned the power of language on that bus trip. Langston Hughes's poem touched this student in a significant way. The words and rhythms were integrated into his being until he had to share them with others. A lesson that I thought of as just a fun activity took on depth, transcending my plans and expectations. I got a firsthand look at the importance of learning styles, interactive lessons, and lessons that encourage creative interpretations of text. The importance of spending time on literature became more evident. Sometimes, weighted down by standards and testing, I focus on covering so much material that I set aside lessons that take a lot of time or seem more like play than learning. Things that can't be tested or assessed in traditional ways seem less important than ones that can. But because students were so engaged in this poem I spent longer on this performance than usual. It was the first year we performed the poetry for other classes. We added props and costumes. Now I know that time spent to learn things deeply is as, if not more, important than covering vast amounts of content. I continue to teach lessons that provide only a taste, a touch, but I also have lessons which encourage deep learning.

Today this lesson keeps me in tune with the interests and talents of my students. I provide many ways for students to demonstrate their understanding of literature, including art, drama, movement, writing, and speaking. We celebrate literature. We perform Lewis Carroll's "Jabberwocky," and when Science classes are studying insects, we perform Paul Fleischman's "Fireflies." It is not unusual for a former student, upon seeing me in the grocery store, to call out "'Twas brillig and the slithy toves" or tell me they studied Langston Hughes in college freshman English. These are the memories and learning that stick. Literature becomes our common bond and I can think of no greater aspiration.

For the past half-dozen years I've been assisting teachers in their professional development as they work toward achieving National Board Certification. I can't think of a better job, helping teachers who in turn work with students. One of the many insights I've gained has been around the purposes of our teaching. What are those "carry-aways," what do we want students to know and be able to do next year, in 5 years, for the rest of their lives? Unfortunately, many teachers don't get it. They go from textbook chapter to textbook chapter, from lesson to lesson without thinking about what is important and meaningful for students to know. They're encouraged by some education policies to continue to cover the curriculum without taking the time for the reflection that will help them make better choices. They are frequently the teachers whose students don't find the relevance in what they're expected to learn and hence don't learn it very well or for very long. The teachers whose stories appear on these pages are not among them. These teachers, like Kathleen González, know that studying literature is not about memorizing the authors and titles, it's learning about conflict and how people work through the problems they encounter. Thanks to the strategies she chose, the students in Kathleen's classes will always be able to empathize with others, to see life through others' perspectives and to grow as compassionate citizens. We won't ever measure these qualities on a test; the measurement will come over time in how they live their lives.

Blueberry Stains

Kathleen González

Blueberry stains. That's one vivid image in my mind, that and the smell of musty muslin, 50 years old, sweaty with the scent of terror. The blueberry stains formed a Star of David on the concentration camp prisoner's armband, one fashioned quickly out of fear of being caught without this requirement. Katie passed the armband around the room in a ziplock bag, telling us the story of how it had been made from left-over ink and blueberries picked in the fields. She later explained that her grandfather had received the armband from a Jewish family he had met when his troop liberated a concentration camp.

But Katie told the story of this armband in the first person point of view, as if it were her own experience. Students had each chosen two characters from Elie Wiesel's *Night*, a Jewish and a non-Jewish one, and then wrote first-person narratives about their lives during the war. What was their family or home life like? What did they experience during the Holocaust? What were their hopes and dreams for the future? Students then presented one persona to the class, along with an artifact of their own creation. Artifacts included crumpled and burned poems from a concentration camp prisoner, Elie's journal, a family photo album with captions. Katie had brought the armband.

I had been teaching *Night* to my high school freshmen for a number of years, engaging students and often awaking in them a hunger for more information on the Holocaust. But I had always been dissatisfied with assessing them on it. An objective test felt wrong; these were real people's lives, not suitable for *Jeopardy* questions. I had recently learned more about backward mapping, the idea that we set objectives, create the assessment, and then plan instruction to help students meet those objectives. It was something I had done occasionally by default but not intentionally by design. What did I want students to know and be able to do? My main objective for this unit was empathy, an understanding of what people experienced during the Holocaust. If I were successful in building empathy, then students would be driven to discover more on their own.

In order to prepare students to write their first-person narratives, I had to build some subskills and background information. I showed a video of the liberation of Bergen-Belsen and of testimonies from camp survivors, prisoners of war, and Allied and Nazi soldiers. Students examined camp prisoner identity cards from the National Holocaust Museum. But my greatest discovery was that Holocaust survivor and author Alicia Appleman-Jurman lived in our community and would happily speak to my class. In preparation for her visit, many students avidly read her book, *Alicia: My Story*, after finishing *Night*. They asked her numerous questions about her life.

For some students, however, even meeting a survivor wasn't as powerful as writing from that perspective themselves, which moved many of them to tears. In a myriad of ways, students connected their reading to real people, real experiences, and real emotions. Their narratives were chilling, moving, and inspiring. We heard from Elie's sister Tzipora, who died her first day at Auschwitz. We heard from a young German man forced into the army, sickened at having to kill. We heard the hatred in a Nazi's voice. We heard from Elie's friend Juliek as his violin was crushed and from Madame Schachter's son seeing his mother beaten for her hallucinations of fire while she was in the boxcar. These were the roles the students wrote and performed.

But the blueberry stains were real.

It didn't matter that Katie hadn't created this artifact herself; its authenticity was like an electric shock. Classmates handled it with reverence, and Katie's voice shook as she read her narrative. Katie had known before of her grandfather's war artifact, but it was her incorporation of it into a first-person narrative that brought history to life for her. A talented though inconsistent student previously, she now burned with a new fire, turning in work early and exceeding requirements. Empathy, the ability to feel another's pain, had roared to life within her.

Try though we might, some students are resistant to learning. We prepare lessons, we learn new strategies, but nothing seems to work. Math teachers may have it the hardest of all, especially with their female students. So many young girls somewhere along the way got the message that girls can't do math—it may have been that Barbie doll. Mark Ellis persisted in his efforts to help Lisa pass Math class, and it worked. Very ordinary interventions, like a phone call home, can have amazing repercussions. For the most part, parents really do want to help. Sometimes they just don't know what to do. For many of our parents, schools aren't friendly places so they don't consider teachers as their partners. We need more exchanges like Mark had with Lisa's father to change all that. Knowing how to teach so students can learn means more than just pedagogy. It may mean engaging a parent, and it always involves caring.

The Phone Call

Mark Ellis

Lisa was one of those students whom adults—parents and teachers alike—might easily overlook. She was generally quiet in class, never out of line, but never really engaged either. She mostly completed most of her work. What stood out was her devotion to her boyfriend. Every paper she handed in had several variations of the pledge "Lisa loves Mike 4-ever" scrawled along the margins. The trouble was, it seemed to me, that Lisa spent much more time thinking about Mike than about mathematics. A natural thing to do, I suppose, as a junior in high school. Again, this could have easily been dismissed as something that I shouldn't be concerned with, especially given the fact that I was teaching a remedial-level Math class. Nonetheless, I was concerned that Lisa was missing work and determined to do something about it.

It was 7:15 in the morning when Lisa came staggering in to my classroom. She opened with, "Thanks for calling my dad." I had called home the night before and told him that I was worried Lisa might be having trouble understanding the work we were doing since she had not turned in three of the last five assignments. I always try to give students the benefit of the doubt when I place such calls. Because I was concerned with Lisa's understanding of the Math curriculum, I gained her father's positive support.

The atmosphere slowly thawed over the next few mornings when Lisa arrived early for tutoring. We reviewed some of the math problems from previous assignments. I discovered in working with her that Lisa was very quick to catch on to conceptual generalizations but that she lacked the confidence to follow these insights. After each problem, she would call me over for my approval. It became a joke between us when I would say with exasperation, "What? All correct? You're making my job too easy!"

For a while the morning visits became something of a regular occurrence, by Lisa's choosing. She found it a good, quiet space in which to complete her work. Less and less did I find myself being summoned to check her work. By the second semester, Lisa was the top student in my class. Her energy in the classroom encouraged other students to become more involved in the activities we did. I marveled at her new attitude but did not understand the significance of the change until I got a call from her father one day. He said he wanted to thank me for motivating him to try again to get Lisa to care about her school work. He explained that for a time he had given up fighting that battle because she was so resistant. I could hear the smile in his voice as he told me that instead of threatening to drop out of school, Lisa was now talking to him about wanting to continue on to junior college after graduation to earn a degree in computer science.

Lisa went on the next year to earn straight A's, including the highest grade in her algebra class. The last letter I got from her indicated that she had finished the junior college program and was working at a high-tech company designing Web pages. Oh, and she and Mike were engaged! I guess some things will never change.

There are teachers who study history chronologically, year by year, fact by fact. In high school World History it's not unusual to stop at WWII because the semester is over and that's as far as the teacher got in the textbook. There are other teachers who concentrate on pulling the big ideas out of history, the major themes that recur again and again. Renée O'Brien is one of those. She guided her eighth graders through a study of Genocide and Charismatic Leaders—a topic that is contemporary as well as historical. To make their studies more meaningful, and to provide an audience beyond the classroom, she insisted each student enter an essay in the Scholastic Art and Writing Contest. When teachers set and maintain high standards for themselves and their students, but remain flexible in the execution, wonderful things can happen.

The Forgotten Holocaust

Renée O'Brien

As a teacher of gifted eighth graders I was met with a lot of opposition from the students when I insisted they enter the Scholastic Art and

Writing Contest. One student vehemently protested that he was not a writer and that he had nothing to write about. This particular student was highly gifted and had a particular interest in world religions. He had questioned me extensively about my own religion, Judaism. He liked the similarities Judaism had to his own Buddhist faith. When it came close to time to turn in his entry he insisted he was incapable of writing a suitable piece. I encouraged him to write about something close to his heart. I suggested using his fascination with rap music to shape a poem. He laughed at the idea that poetry was music without instruments.

We were in the middle of a unit called Genocide and Charismatic Leaders, which focused on the psychology behind dictators and the extreme level of intolerance they provoked in implementing a genocidal plan. We had spent several classes discussing Hitler, Pol Pot, Mussolini, and others. Virak told stories of his parents' exodus from Pol Pot's regime. He was passionate about their suffering and his ire was palpable. I suggested he use some of that emotion to write.

He questioned his parents and did research on the Internet, which he often shared with us during class discussions. He didn't mention his writing again for several weeks. The classroom discussions focused on the mental anguish inflicted on a trusting populace and the power of propaganda to hide atrocities from the world. Before and after class he rapped with his friends and used break dancing as a physical outlet. For his daily journal entries he wrote short rap pieces that expressed whatever was on his mind that day. I continued to point out the similarities between rap and poetry. I suggested he read some William Carlos Williams, Shel Silverstein, and others. I pointed out lyrics from popular songs that were especially poetic.

On the due date for the assignment he handed me a poem, making the comment that it wasn't really ready and he'd like to work on it some more. Reading the poem I realized that he had put all of his emotions and sensitivities into this piece of writing, creating strong visual images. The next day I told him that the poem needed no work and I wanted to submit it as it was; he reluctantly agreed.

Several months went by before the results of the county-wide portion of the contest were released. I had many winners that year, and Virak's poem received a first place award for the "American Voice" portion of the contest. His piece went on to the national competition. I submitted all of the pieces that had won to my principal for his perusal. He called me down to his office that afternoon to inform me that he didn't believe a 13-year-old could create such an insightful and moving piece of writing. I knew in my heart that Virak had written the poem but I questioned him anyway to assuage my principal's concerns. Virak was insulted but after some discussion he said that his father could verify that he had written the poem, which he did.

The contest was all but forgotten as we approached the end of the school year. Then the national results were announced. Virak received an "American Voice" award and was invited to a symposium of writers in Washington, D.C. At the end of the year Virak stopped in to see me and told me that he was glad he had entered the contest and that he would never forget me. The passion and emotion embraced by his poem were all the thanks I needed.

I've included Virak's poem here, although it is long, in its entirety. Virak's family and Scholastic have graciously given permission. The poem served as a reminder to me how valuable it is to encourage students to build on their own experiences, to go with their passions, and to draw meaning from their past and from the collective experiences of others. While not all of your students will have had the experience Virak's family had, they will have had other experiences, or know of others, or have an interest in others—if we allow it. Facts taught in isolation, without connection, remain isolated facts quickly forgotten. But when we connect to what students already know or can imagine, we build knowledge that remains as the glue for continued learning. In addition, note the power of having your students submit their work for outside audiences. I've long believed that when the teacher is the only audience for students' work, there is less incentive to perform at high levels. When we use the community as an audience, be it formal contests or local publishing, we tell students that what they say and do is important and valued. Motivation increases and quality definitely goes up. There are numerous sources online for student publishing. Ask students to find them and you'll all be winners.

The Forgotten Holocaust

Virak

Can you taste it? Can you taste it in the air?
The unforgettable bitterness of which we call despair.
As millions were murdered in the land of the Khmer.
A genocide, which sits in history gathering dust.
Most can't recall the battle's deathly must.
As my people lay unremembered a drop in the ocean
It seems that mass murder causes little commotion.
In a world desensitized by everyday death.
Can you smell it? Can you smell the dying's last breath?
Skulls scattered in ponds and sown in soil,
And from the world was little recoil.
For years people suffered in the fields of the killing,
Just another body, just some more blood spilling.
Blood on the hands of he who dare grip mortality;
His name Pol Pot the man with the greatest audacity.
The brother who killed hundreds of his own kin,
He has no remorse morbid signs of a grin.
To claim he works for the good of a nation
Lives just a minor consequence in his "brilliant" reformation
People just eggs who will inevitably be broken,
Each killing is just natural like words being spoken.
Groups, no crowds, lined up to be murdered.
Eight people with one shot so less bullets need be ordered.
Drowning them in puddles and beating them with batons,
His soldiers, children of death and pitiless drones.
Young boys killing women as old as their mother,
Blinded by loyalty not realizing it's each other.
Killing children and babies and mothers and fathers.
My sister. Your brother. Their sons. Our daughters.
Undiscriminating murder and rapes and beatings were
    common.
And if they tried to plea for mercy it would be no problem.
Just sit them in a pond and tie a bag over their head.

And you can't talk now if you're dead.
Imagine a mother watching the death of her children,
Tied up with flesh burning rope and skinny with malnutrition.
Their toes salted and cut open with a dirty knife.
Picture when the four letter word P-A-I-N becomes
    your life.
Can you see it? Can you comprehend being tortured as
    they laugh?
Now imagine walking through a pattie and hearing a
    jagged crack.
You lift your foot to find your brother's broken bones,
Didn't even know he had died and to find out in this tone.
You were talking with him, ago, it was not long.
He was obviously killed while you were gone.
You shut his eyelids and untie a cord around his neck,
You hold back the tears so the soldiers won't check.
So they won't see and kill you too.
You ask him for forgiveness then rip out a gold tooth.
The gold will help you feed your very sick mom,
Giving her strength to run away with you
From the land that you call home.
She's too old as it is to work under these conditions,
Suffering from arthritis, a debilitating position.
You work and think about the Nixon Breakfast Operation,
    which dropped tons of napalm shells.
In fact they're probably the reason for the war itself.
Can you hear it? The screams of children and infants as
    you run through the jungle.
Sneaking out at night and this time the trouble's double.
You're reassured for a second not hearing a thing.
But then it fires out an explosive ring.
A mine, a souvenir from the Vietnam war,
Killing two infants and a boy, mutilated remains splash on
    the floor.
A mother runs to the children and lifts her babies' heads;
Frantically yelling and screaming trying to wake them
    from dead.
Her tears stream down as she cradles them next to her chin.
Later killing herself to join her babies again.
On the way, your mother dies of pneumonia and cold,

Now you look back on the story that your life has told.
You lived a life of hell, burning, agonizing and rotten,
To only wake up to see the genocidal horror has been
     forgotten.
How does that feel?

I just reread Virak's poem and understand now even more deeply the power of literature to help us to understand—everything. I need to take a mental break, to absorb Virak's words and experiences, especially in light of more recent acts of war and terrorism in the Middle East. I need some wait time about now before moving on to another moving experience where literature takes us back to another time and place.

There is much controversy in education circles about the value of the standards. There are books claiming that one size doesn't fit all (Ohanian, 1999) and others on making standards work (Reeves, 2001, 2002). I think that having standards is critically important. They provide a blueprint for students. They need to know, in advance, what they will be expected to do and know over a period of time. Teachers need that blueprint as well. What do I expect students to know and be able to do by the end of the semester or year? What lessons will I teach, what strategies will I use, to help students to master the standards? Although the standards can provide an excellent directional blueprint, they can also bog us down. I've been in many classrooms only to see a standard written in educationese on the board, and the teacher telling students they will be working on this or that standard for the period or day. It's even worse when on the front board there's a listing, Standard 2.3, with no explanation at all. Clearly, the teacher doesn't get it and for sure the students won't either.

When the standards are examined as a whole, when the big ideas are pulled out, and when teachers take ownership, then anything can happen. The standards are nothing to be afraid of. They are freeing, not restricting, and they can be anything but standard. The Language

Arts strands, for example, of listening, speaking, reading, and writing, can be woven into lessons that make literature come alive—in the hands of an accomplished teacher. Snap your fingers. Listen to the jazz playing in the background, dim the lights, and read on as we join Jeanne Owens's class at their Harlem coffeehouse. You be the judge of whether the standards are being met.

An Emotional Response

Jeanne Owens

My middle school Language Arts class is an elective course for seventh- and eighth-grade students who qualify as gifted and talented. My students choose to take GATEway because of the academic challenge it provides and the enrichment experiences they receive as participants. This school year my students and I operated under the theme of "Taking a Stand and Affecting Change." Middle school students understand change; they are constantly encountering changes within themselves emotionally, physically, intellectually, and socially. Using change as a theme was a perfect fit. Through this theme, students opened to the idea that change can be positive, good, and necessary if a world, country, community, school, or person desires to continue to grow, learn, and evolve. Just as adolescence is not an easy time of growth and change, neither is it ever easy for a person to take a stand and affect change when faced with opposition.

During one particular unit of study we explored the stand taken by a group of artists, writers, and musicians in order to create a new image of African Americans that emerged from the time of the Harlem Renaissance. We arranged the room in order for students to experience the atmosphere of a poetry reading in a Harlem coffeehouse. The chairs were in a circle with small tables around the room, lamps were brought in to provide soft lighting, jazz music of the era played quietly in the background, and students sipped hot chocolate as we examined, analyzed, and wrote poetry for three days. We spent the first day reading the poetry of selected writers: Langston Hughes, James Weldon Johnson, Margaret Walker, Gwendolyn Brooks, Angelina Grimke, and

Gwendolyn Bennett. We read poems aloud, discussed them as a group, and then students read them a second time. When we finished all the selections from one poet, we talked about the differences in the poems, the things they had in common, and how that poet differed from the others. We discussed the mood and tone from which the poet seemed to write. Students began identifying that it wasn't a certain style or type of poem that bound these poets together. Ashley observed, "It's more a mood that was used, a written-from-the-gut type poetry." They began to hear the rhythm of jazz music in the poetry, to visualize Lennox Avenue, and to feel the pain of death and prejudice in the words. Jaspm said, "The poetry feels raw and rough, but it's beautiful at the same time." They understood. The second day in the coffeehouse students spent writing poems in the style of one of the poets we examined. They sipped hot chocolate as jazz music played softly. They shared ideas quietly from coffee table to coffee table. They moved about using standard dictionaries and the rhyming dictionary on the Internet as they worked on their poems.

Throughout the entire three days we spent in our classroom-turned-coffeehouse, I was taken aback by the way students responded to literature, to writing, and to each other. Day 3 was set aside for sharing original poetry. I came away from these readings with a lump in my throat and a rock in the pit of my stomach. They shared. They shared deeply and it was both painful and natural for them. By the time the last hour of the day rolled around, I was completely overwhelmed by the interaction. Students volunteered to read as they felt comfortable. That hour, Bailey indicated that she was ready. Before she began reading, Bailey tentatively said, "I guess I kind of based my poem on Johnson's 'The Glory of the Day Was in Her Face' because I used that same rhyme scheme and the same mood." When Bailey finished reading her poem the class began to snap—an applause technique students learned was used in Harlem coffeehouses—they jumped on it and insisted we use it too. Claire was the first to comment, "I liked it at first, because of how she kind of went through everything—like the person she's speaking about just went to work for the day, like she was just being left with a sitter. But then it moved from childhood to adulthood, it became bigger as it moved. Bigger and sadder." At that point Brandy slipped into the discussion with, "It even went all the way to death! She took you all the way through the mother's life." Anna added, "It surprised me. I wasn't expecting it to go that way at all." Bailey read her poem a second time. We listened, we snapped, and I asked, "Who's next?"

Little did I know what was about to occur when Steven spoke up with, "I'll read. I really didn't base it on one of the poets," he admitted, "because I had a phone call last night, and I based it on that." Then Steven began to read his poem about a friend wanting to die. Halfway through his poem Steven began to cry. The two girls sitting across from Steven were suddenly also in tears; another reached for the tissues. My class was falling apart emotionally. Steven finished his poem and the mom in me went over to hug him. I had to acknowledge what had just happened in a different way. Steven understood the original assignment. He had written the beginning of another poem in class the day before; a poem that did follow the instructions. The poem Steven chose to share in our reading was a glimpse of the much bigger picture of what teaching Language Arts is all about. It was written as a response to strong feelings and then shared and validated in a safe place. It was a beautiful example of what learning should be.

We listened to the remaining student poems, and then as a group we discussed our experience in order to pull it all together. I asked, "What does this group hold within?" The answers amazed me. Brandy responded that the group was serious, and had taken the assignment very seriously, and that doesn't happen in all classes. Ashley said the word "Passion." Then she added, "Not like a love passion, but more of a passion for life and for what is inside of us all." Jimmy then said, "This group holds great expression." I thought they had said it all.

The strands of Language Arts were evident and alive. I loved watching it happen in a way that moved students so strongly. There was energy in the room, and it revolved around expressing their thoughts and feelings in writing. It was one of those magic moments as a teacher when you sit back in awe, breathe deeply, and just allow it to flow. It was a moment I did not create; no lesson plan could have produced that kind of openness—it was simply a moment of which I was part and I'm honored to have been.

In recent years there's been a call to the public sector inviting retired and mid-career professionals to join the teaching force. The underlying premise is that if one knows a subject, like engineers know math or chemists know chemistry, then one would make a great teacher. But experienced teachers know that isn't so. Only about 20%

of student achievement comes from teachers' content knowledge, while nearly 50% can be attributed to teachers' repertoire of strategies, the teacher's tool box. There isn't another profession that encourages untrained practitioners. Could you imagine having former airline pilots do laser surgery on your eyes because they know how to use mechanical equipment? Marcia Harris' story about a student who couldn't seem to master the multiplication tables and the extraordinary lengths she went to in order to help him succeed underscores how complex great teaching really is. Accomplished teaching really is brain surgery. Those who can teach, do.

"Way Out" But Wonderful and Worth It

Marcia Harris

During my 30 years of teaching I have tried various methods to help students to master concepts, some traditional and some quite unusual. Here's one that was way out, wonderful, and worth it.

Five years ago, Carl, a third-grade student, felt like a failure. He looked at the task of learning the multiplication tables as a death sentence. His father, his Math teacher, and Carl were all frustrated. Punishments, bribes, and worksheets didn't work. Carl shut down and didn't care anymore. During a conference Carl blurted out that there was no way he could learn the multiplication tables and no reason to do so. His father remarked that he couldn't help his son because all he knew was woodwork. I knew Carl did not feel valued. I wanted a way for him to feel important, to learn the times tables, and to improve the father–son relationship. An idea flashed into my head. I had always wanted to build a magic illusion that I saw as a child on the *Mr. Wizard* TV show, but I had no idea how to build it or what tools I'd need.

Tears dripped down Carl's face. I reacted with, "I have an idea!" Both father and son were listening. I told them that we could build a secret magic illusion and learn the tables at the same time. I explained that I could come after school or on the weekends to his home to work with them building this illusion that would, at a later date, be used to showcase Carl's head reciting the math facts. Both father and son, although puzzled, perked up. We developed a game plan. Carl would write to a magician for the directions and to companies for the supplies. (Both the magician and the company responded.) We began the building project and as we worked we practiced the times tables. It became a special secret. Neighbors watched and wondered while we worked. Before long, Carl was feeling proud of his father, our project, and himself. Carl's father realized he used more math in his woodwork than he realized, and I learned how to build my illusion. Carl learned many things, including the times tables.

We spread the word around school that on June 8th classes could come to see Mrs. Harris cut Carl's head off. It was the talk of the school. The illusion was beautifully constructed—a quality showpiece. The curtain opened to a full auditorium. Carl's classmates said, "Mrs. Harris made us work our heads off learning the times tables." There in the center was a round table topped with a tray and Carl's head on the tray. Carl's head twisted from side to side as classmates quizzed him on the facts. He shouted the correct answers. The four legs of the table were completely visible, but only Carl's head and neck showed. Everyone was confused, wondering where the body went. We never told.

The magic trick brought magic into Carl's life in more ways than one. His relationship with his father improved and now, years later, Carl is a top junior high Math student. When he came back to visit he told me that every time he does a math problem he thinks of his head on the tray twisting away from side to side.

TV's *Mr. Wizard* from my childhood inspired my curiosity and that illusion allowed Carl to master the multiplication tables, not just in an illusion but also in reality. This strategy had a different "twist" to learning the times tables and making an impact on student learning.

Most of us are pretty wedded to our curriculum. There are subjects we like to teach, books we've personally enjoyed and want to pass on, and science experiments that are easy to set up or break down. Like everyone else's, our habits provide some comfort, a routine we don't have to think about too much. Unfortunately, we sometimes forget that we teach students, not curriculum; that each class has its own personality and presents its own challenges; and that the world beyond our classrooms is in constant flux. The tension remains regarding how to teach what we enjoy, because learning is enhanced when we teach to our passions, and how to satisfy district requirements and still meet the needs of individual students. It's not easy to achieve the right balance. Sometimes we get very lucky and we're able to apply the curriculum creatively in order to meet students where they are and hook them in by connecting with their interests. Not all of us can float a head on a table or create a Harlem coffee scene, but each of us can listen to students, learn about their interests, and use those interests to open the door to academic learning.

I recently worked with a second-year teacher who already has recognized the joy of running with the teachable moment. Athena teaches a secondary reading intervention class and sometimes struggles with the requirements. One Friday, in lieu of the regular curriculum, and behind a closed door, she asked her students, all struggling readers, what they wanted to know. She listed their questions: "What is the aurora borealis? Why are we going to war with Iraq? What causes earthquakes?" Then, in one of those teachable moments, she broke them into six groups, one group for each class computer, and allowed them to find the answers to one of the questions. In 50 minutes they had to pick some key words for an Internet search, get information on their subject from at least three sources, read what they found, and then report their findings to the rest of the class without reading from the Net, just from notes they had made. They did it. This was a class of struggling secondary readers but they read and synthesized information from three different sources! Maybe they struggle only when they're not engaged, when they don't see the relevance of what they've been asked to do. I also taught struggling readers at an urban high school. We read *Native Son*. We read some out loud, some individually and silently, and we had lots of conversations about the text. They were engaged, enthralled, and motivated. Great teaching means we catch them where they are. That's what Maureen Robinson did to entice Shawn, one of our future comics, into reading and writing.

Even Comedians Need to Write

Maureen Robinson

Allow me to introduce you to Shawn, a seventh grader who thrives on humor and comedy. His role model is comedian John Leguizamo, whom, I must confess, I had never heard of. Since the first semester, Shawn professed time and time again that comedy was his future. He envisioned himself on stage, a purveyor of one-liners, ad-libs, and impromptu stories. He didn't make any connection between school and his future goal. When questioned how a comedy routine is developed and orchestrated, Shawn said that comedy routines are the impromptu design of the creator. He didn't connect scripting to writing. With a straight face and deadpan attitude, I told him high quality on-stage performances required strong writing skills. Laughing, he responded, "A comedian doesn't need to have writing skills. They just tell jokes off the top of their heads." He didn't see that jokes were designed, edited, and delivered after much painstaking writing effort.

During Language Arts, I hoped to demonstrate a parallel between writing comedic routines and routine class writing assignments. I made an effort to relate Shawn's interest in comedy to writing, pointing out that his comedic idol had to have a beginning, middle, and closing for each performance. All joking aside, my goal was for Shawn to see the obvious correlation between comedy and the writing process. Shawn was not buying it. His paragraph writing was a rambling disjointed stream of consciousness. His writing skills were weak, lacking in mechanics and organization. A piece on the population crisis in China traveled from one-child families to land use to laws created, but who knew for what, either the family or the land. Shawn was not yet a believer in the value of writing, so the comedic connection lay fallow.

It was a long first semester when piece after piece was edited and revised. Shawn continued to laugh at the language, put apostrophes on every word that ended with *s*, and expressed an aw-shucks attitude to improving. The New Year, third semester, arrived, and I assigned an essay. The topic was to draft, revise, and finalize an essay on a resolution for the New Year. Shawn announced his resolution to be a comedian again. A groan went up around the room. But, the groan was followed by a challenge: go for it, prove it to us, but do it in a properly formatted essay style.

Miracles do occur. His essay was drafted, in a glorious outline form. His final was revised and edited magnificently. His organization scrolled from an introduction, to three body paragraphs concerning the joys of comedy, and a pride-filled conclusion. In the first body paragraph he expressed his reasons for loving comedy. From his desire to make people laugh and happy, he expressed how the joy of their laughter filled him with a sense of warmth. Of course, Shawn finished that paragraph with a brash stroke that if he made people laugh, "I could get famous."

In his second body paragraph he listed steps for achieving his goal: study comedic styles, acquire a wealth of material, use his uncle as a model. His finishing body paragraph discussed the pride he would feel upon this achievement. He concluded with his willingness to strive and work hard. He expressed confidence in his ability to reach his dream. He did it. He had a beginning, a middle, and an end. He used supporting arguments, he was sincere and genuine, and his classmates listened like they never had before. Shawn's audience, his classmates, applauded. And I felt like a winner also for helping Shawn acquire one of the skills he would need in order to be a successful comic.

You're doing all the right things. You build on prior knowledge that you carefully uncover. You work to connect the curriculum to subjects the students find interesting. You allow students to choose from a range of assignments. Once your classes become student focused, you don't have complete control. Students will surprise you. They astound you by how much they know and by how much they know about things far removed from your own experiences. And they surprise you with their candor and their honesty. When I hear people, educators and others, complain that students don't want to learn, that they're unmotivated, I think about kids like Gina who come to school against odds that would stop many adults.

Getting to Know Gina

Catherine Humphrey

Gina seemed incapable of sitting in her chair for more than 15 minutes at a time. Even when in her chair, she was fidgety, looking in her makeup bag, drawing raspberry colored clown lips on her mouth, working with eyeliner. Her hair color varied—bright pink, yellow, black, currently brown. She had to be reminded to take her feet off the desk, to stop talking across the room. Gina did not demonstrate appropriate behavior for success as a high school sophomore. After receiving an assignment, as other students began work, Gina would shout out, "But what are we supposed to do?" I moved her seat from one side of the room to another, from front to back. It made little difference. She still roamed around way too often, talked too loudly at the wrong times. How might I channel Gina's energy into more productive, less disruptive student behavior? After students read John Steinbeck's *Grapes of Wrath* and wrote several papers, including a piece on Dorothea Lange's portrait of the "The Migrant Mother," I asked students to create their own photo essay. They chose an issue in their own communities that they felt passionately about, created an argumentative thesis, and took their own photographs to illustrate their papers. Students then made oral presentations and turned their photo-essays in for assessment.

Gina was immediately enthused. She asked if she could write her essay on the homeless. She wrote the following thesis statement: "Despite what people may see when they look at me and the clothes I wear or the way I act, I know what it is like to have no roof over my head, no money in my pocket, and no food in my stomach, because I have experienced all of that stuff." She continued, "Most people do not understand how hard it is to be a person in poverty." She took photos of a run-down neighborhood, the Hope Homeless Shelter, and a man pushing a shopping cart filled with clothes and a blanket, plastic sacks tied to the wire sides and handle. She wrote, "When I went to take pictures, many people would turn away because they do not need more people to look down on them. They have to hide out in dark places like allies, behind big buildings, and even in trash cans." She asked, "I know that the cart is not theirs to take, but what else are they supposed to carry all of their things around in?" Referring to the Hope Homeless Shelter, she argued, "This is a place where people can reach out and find help. There should be a few more of these around.... Homeless deserve the chance to get a fresh new start in their lives." Next to photos of trash yards, she wrote, "Less fortunate children have no toys so they find other ways to entertain themselves like building up trash and playing in it." Gina volunteered first to read her photo essay and show her pictures to the class. She read, "People think that it can't be that hard to live on the street. Well, they can't say that unless they have been there, and I have. There is a difference in just hearing about how it is to be living on the streets and to actually experience it. I have been there, and let me tell you, it is not a place to be. It seems that when you live on the streets you lose all of your dignity and respect for yourself. You would do anything for food or a warm place to sleep." She suggested that her classmates go through their closets and take the clothes they do not need to a nearby shelter, offer to feed a poor family, "put them up in a hotel for a night,...give someone pushing a cart a quarter or a dollar because I know they would be grateful," and "you will have the satisfaction of knowing that you made their day a little easier."

Gina read with a strong voice. When she held her essay and mounted pictures up for the class to see, the students applauded. Gina's paper provided a key into her world that helps me understand her classroom behavior. I use this information to provide nurture as well as instruction, safety as well as appropriate risk taking, praise for work well done as well as guidance.

Gina remains a challenging student. She flits around the room more often than I would like. She talks across the class too frequently and she is often disruptive, but last Wednesday, her final exam, a complex 2-hour analytical in-class essay, earned one of the few A's. I can't wait to see her face when I return her paper with the blue ribbon I reserve for the best work. We will be proud together, and probably the other students will clap.

Accomplished teachers know the subjects they teach and how to teach them so students can learn—or do they? Diane Saienni Albanese had some instructional goals in mind when she began her poetry unit, but with 11- and 12-year-olds, one never knows. Diane's students took their poetry writing very seriously, and their teacher turned out to be another student.

Poetry Lesson

Diane Saienni Albanese

At times in my class it's difficult to tell who the learner is and who the teacher is. On days when students share their writing, I am definitely the learner. Their world, as much as they may wish to share, is opened just a crack and I am allowed to step inside. Last spring the students shared poetry. After writing and revising poetry for several weeks, my sixth-grade students sit in a circle on the carpet and share what they have written. The reading of poetry is very personal; they only read their poem aloud if they choose. At age 11 or 12 they are not always willing to bare their souls or reveal their deepest thoughts.

This day was different. Several students shared their poems about baseball and pesky little brothers. Then came Andrew. Andrew, who unfortunately was failing some of his other classes, read his romantic love poem to the class. He was sincere and completely without self-consciousness. Full of magical preteen angst and wonderment, the poem described a girl with lovely hair, soft skin, and crystal blue eyes. Twelve-year-old Andrew was smitten. As he was reading, the other boys in the class glanced uncomfortably at each other as if Andrew had just crossed over an invisible barrier to another world, another place. The boys squirmed and snickered; the girls giggled. I went with my gut instinct to let him continue all the while thinking I should have preread the poem. What if Andrew had written something lewd? I could picture the parents storming the school demanding that poetry be eliminated from the writing curriculum, picketing the school with signs, "Ban poetry writing! Teachers beware," and it would all be my fault. Yet, I had asked them to write about what was important to them, and they did. Andrew spilled his soul. The poem was almost too difficult for us to bear: the giggling, the anxiety, and the uncertainty of prepubescent blossoming all came together in his love poem. I asked for them to do this—to come clean—to dig down deep—to express their feelings—and then he did it. OH MY GOD.

But what is poetry? I asked them this question in a final quiz at the end of the unit. Now I'm asking myself—all-knowing, all-powerful teacher that I am supposed to be. Poetry is emotion, poetry is the human experience—poetry is a window to your soul. No one who sat in the poetry circle and listened to Andrew's love poem that day was ever the same. The boys and girls in the class began to write differently, more sophisticated, more deeply felt, mature poems. I read their poems with an altered insight into the maturation of young adolescents. Andrew grew about 10 inches taller. He went on to read his love poem over the intercom for the whole school to hear. My expectations for poetry writing have changed. Poetry is a vehicle to allow them to expand their thoughts and ideas, and I can never be quite sure where it will lead. I trusted my students and the process, and there were no pickets, and poetry lives on.

I taught English Language Arts for 13 years, and until I brought audience into the classroom I always fell short of what I wanted my students to be able to do. We can teach the writing process, instructing students to revise, to peer edit, and to revise again. We can mark up their pages ad nauseam, noting every grammatical error and spelling faux pas. It doesn't matter if we use the statement–comment–comment format or explore the six writing traits. Until students have an audience to write for, someone beyond themselves and the teacher, their writing will not be as powerful, or as purposeful, as it becomes when there is an audience. The audience can be fellow students at a Harlem Renaissance-style coffeehouse, a school newspaper, or a group of second graders. Los Angeles teacher Helene Hirsch understands the formula:

Real Products + Real Audiences =
Higher Motivation + Improved Student Achievement

Three Pigs

Helene Hirsch

Beginning in January, students in my sixth-grade English Language Arts class read various versions of *The Three Little Pigs*. We compare and contrast versions told from different viewpoints, written in other languages, and set in different areas of the world. Each student creates a personal version of the fable by following the entire writing process. They each author, illustrate, bind, and publish their very own hard cover book and then read it aloud to younger students at an author's fair.

This has been an exceptional project from many standpoints. Students choose the setting, characters, and plot for their own stories.

The process is long and difficult, a challenge for most of my students, but they have found it to be extremely worthwhile nevertheless. Students really buy-in to the whole process when they realize they use their own experiences as a basis for the book's ideas.

Over the years, many students have written strong stories, but three stories really stand out. Tremaine set his story in downtown Los Angeles. His characters wanted to move to another part of town because of gang-related problems. Tremaine's story had a hard edge to it, especially for a 9-year-old, and it was difficult for me to read objectively. He wrote about how gangs were terrorizing a family and shooting up the neighborhood. The strongest main character in his story was the mother. She held the family together and managed to move them away from the big bad wolf. This was a terrific story indeed, but the most outstanding point was the dedication. He wrote, "I dedicate this book to my cousin Michael who got shot in a drive-by." Tremaine had moved into our neighborhood the previous year; this was his story.

Kyle's book was not as moving, but what it represented in terms of his learning was indeed quite remarkable. Kyle has ADHD [Attention Deficit Hyperactivity Disorder] and runs at a mile a minute. He could orally respond to anything asked of him, but seldom stopped long enough to finish anything he started. He was enthusiastic, extremely bright, and a great talker, but that was not enough for him to be a good academic student. He was failing all of his sixth-grade classes other than Language Arts and had already decided school wasn't for him. But he did have a story to tell. He started the book project with the same level of enthusiasm he began all his assignments. He talked up a storm about what he wanted to do. I provided as much guidance as I possibly could to see that he maintained his excitement and wanted to finish what he had started. It worked; he finished his book. He read it aloud to a second-grade class and when he was done, his face said it all. He had finished what he started. He got rave reviews and was successful. The next year he came back to visit often, still proud of his book. This kind of learning, learning to complete something, is not measured on any test that I know of.

Damian's reading level was below grade level and his mind often wandered; still I wanted him to do a book project just like the rest of the class. Like Kyle, he too rarely finished his regular assignments. When we started this project, it didn't look good. He took a long time to warm up to the idea of doing such an involved project. This wasn't an easy project for Damian. It took a great deal of concentrated effort to stay focused on this task. Each day was a challenge, but he did finish. At the end of the year, I got two letters, one from Damian and one from his mom. Damian wrote, "Mrs. Hirsch said, 'I bet you can think of a great story if you put your mind to it.' My book is very special to me because I gave it my best effort. I dedicated my book to a very special person in my life, my little baby sister. This book is very special."

Damian's mom wrote, "He was focused and eager to do a good job because he feels that he's a good role model for his sister. He knew that one day, when his sister was old enough to read, she would be reading his story. Damian learned that when you take a personal interest in your work, you are able to do a better job. He learned to edit his own work and hand in a completed project that he could be proud of. He learned that a good result requires focus, interest, and a lot of time. Thank you for your imaginative motivation and encouragement that allowed my son to complete a successful project. I am so proud of my son." And that's why I teach. What more is there to say?

I attended a workshop early in my teaching career on the power of words. The presenter began by having us reflect on a time when words hurt us. Every one of us recalled being verbally taunted. We moved from the power of words to taunt us to the power of words to make us feel good. Words are also the keys that allow us to move between different settings—financial, academic, and familial. Students naturally code-switch from their native language, if it's other than English, to English, from classroom speak to playground speak. We know that rich vocabulary as tested on the SATs is critical if one is to be accepted to a 4-year university, but a strong vocabulary serves us well way before and way beyond the college entrance exams. We can open doors for our students by introducing them to the language of power, to a vocabulary that will allow them to express themselves clearly and to communicate, verbally and in writing, effectively. Middle Childhood Generalist Stephanie Penniman didn't think her third graders had to wait until they were in high school before they could begin to use *grown-up* words. She helped them, instead, to become the words.

Grown-Up Language

Stephanie Penniman

I teach at a school in the San Fernando Valley that ranks very low in national test scores due to language, poverty, and other issues that impact inner-city schools. For many of my students, I need to develop important concepts and support their understanding with sheltered English, using the key vocabulary words necessary to help them meet state standards. One day my high school daughter brought home a study book titled, *1100 Words You Need To Know*. I decided to teach some of these college words to my third-grade students—words like *pugnacious, implore, spontaneous*, and *gesticulate*. The children loved the words and proudly came back to school the next day announcing that even their parents didn't know these words. Several of the excited parents wrote notes of encouragement to me to keep it up and said they were pleased to see their children talking about going to college.

After a few months of study, our school principal walked by my class, which was out on the yard. Marisse said, "Ms. Barrett, you look flamboyant." Ms. Barrett laughed and responded with several other study words the children recognized, so I invited her into our classroom to face a vocabulary challenge with my students. She is a brilliant woman with numerous college degrees and credentials herself, so I decided to say only the meaning of each word, and she and the student challenger had to each try to be first to say the correct word hidden on my card. Being a good sport, Ms. Barrett agreed to these rules as long as every single child participated and took a turn. The children won the match, barely, but were so thrilled about winning that we decided to have two other rematches. Everyone studied and felt successful.

In order to personalize the words for the children, I used many of the students as examples to explain the meaning of words like *altruistic, vociferous, pandemonium*, and *fastidious*. They loved this personal connection so much that one day everyone taped a word card to his or her chest and went outside on the yard. Other teachers were impressed with their understanding of these words and praised them for being so smart. One student in particular had a family history of drug abuse and police records. He came to school midyear and was filled with anger. Although he was below grade level in many subjects, he loved the vocabulary words and excelled in this area. His grandmother saw a dramatic change in the boy and said that his attitude about school was completely different. Even after he left my classroom, he continued to ask me for more vocabulary words the following year.

At the end of the semester, I asked the children to write a letter to me stating the one or two most valuable things they had learned during the school year. Many of them said the vocabulary words were the most important, because "now I can go to college!"

We learn best when the material we're attempting to learn is timely and relevant. I am a voracious consumer of education research at this time in my career, but I rarely examine the political scene. Both can be very interesting, but as the consumer I am determining what is relevant and timely for me to know. Our students don't generally have that freedom of choice. We determine the curriculum, what will be taught, and when it will be tested. We therefore have the responsibility of making the material relevant to our students' lives. In general, we haven't done a very good job of helping students to make connections between classroom learning and the world beyond the schoolhouse doors. There is a great difference between adhering to a standard that states, "All students will assess the likely causes of the Great Depression and analyze its effect on ordinary people in different parts of the nation" and in addressing it by making it relevant so students will want to learn about the Depression.

Take this standard and put it in the hands of an accomplished teacher, as James O. Lee does in his article in the February 2003 issue of the *Phi Delta Kappan*. Lee suggests that teachers must ask, "To what extent will my students be ready to engage the standard in light of their previous learning and understandings?" (Lee, 2003). The social studies standard on the Great Depression then becomes, "In what ways might the lives and experiences of my students connect to the experiences of those who suffered through the Great Depression? What sense will students make of the Depression in the context of their own poverty?" The standards are not inherently good or bad, relevant or not relevant. In the hands of a skilled practitioner, everything can be interesting and relevant. When we are reflective, when we ask the tough questions, such as, "Do I care whether students' understanding of the Depression is only superficial or is developed in some depth?" and "How will the answers to these questions differ with different students?" then we help students find meaning and relevance in the curriculum. They are more engaged, classroom management becomes a nonissue, and everyone wins.

Helene Hirsch designed her classroom management system around the free-enterprise economy enjoyed in the United States. She taught Economics 101 to her third-grade students by having them live it. Not only were they enthusiastic participants, but they took what they were learning in class and incorporated the principles into their lives beyond the class.

Economics 101

Helene Hirsch

Economics is a subject rarely discussed among third graders, yet it is of the utmost value. My students get to study economics up-close and quite personally. In my third-grade class students kept ledgers on their desks to track daily income and expenditures. They earn and spend money based upon school performance. They deposit paychecks, balance checkbooks, and pay weekly bills. We discuss necessities versus luxuries. They deal with the effects of their spending decisions. They experience rewards, repossessions, and homelessness depending upon how well they have learned to budget their assets. Developing these real-life skills is a very important part of their education. I didn't realize quite how important until two events occurred.

The first event was a conversation I had with a student's aunt. The class was learning how to fill out checks and check registers. Ian really took the lessons to heart. He went home and heard his aunt complaining about her checkbook and then volunteered to help. He claimed to be able to solve her problems. She was skeptical at first, but allowed him to try. Her skepticism turned to excitement when Ian successfully balanced her checkbook. She was thrilled and so was he. She said she would give him the job every month.

The second event was a call from the principal. Michael and Travis got into some difficulties on the yard. Apparently, Travis lent Michael some of our classroom money because he was short of funds and was about to be classified as homeless. His desk and chair were in danger of being repossessed. To pay some of his classroom bills, he talked Travis into making him a loan. Travis wrote Michael a check so that he could pay for his weekly desk and chair rental. (Remember, this money does not really exist outside of the classroom; I didn't actually charge students rent for their desks and chairs.) Two weeks passed and Michael still hadn't repaid the loan. Since the class store opened every two weeks, Travis wanted to buy some items from the store but didn't have the money because Michael still hadn't paid off his loan. Their schoolyard discussion became quite animated. The boys were eventually removed from the yard and sent to the principal's office.

The wise principal, already briefed on our classroom monetary system, offered Michael an opportunity to earn back the money he borrowed. He could earn a salary by picking up trash on the yard. The salary would equal the amount he owed Travis. Michael worked off his debt and the principal paid him. He gave the money to Travis. Travis bought the items he wanted from the class store. It was an incredible learning experience all the way around. We had long discussions. We talked about never loaning any money that you cannot afford to give away freely. We discussed the responsibility of repaying your debts on time. We conferred about the need to budget your resources to be able to meet your obligations. Everyone involved learned some truly valuable lessons this day. And along the way they learned Economics 101.

Over the past few years many of our urban schools have adopted scripted reading programs. The theory is that if teachers only have to read a script, then every student would get access to the same curriculum. I attended one of the trainings offered by a scripted textbook publisher where the facilitator said, "This is designed so teachers don't have to think. We don't want them to think." It was difficult for me to remain silent, but I did. It's true that many students have suffered unnecessarily because their primary teachers didn't know how to teach them to read. Many of these students would have benefited from a scripted reading program, but they would have benefited even more if the monies and time taken to teach teachers to use the scripted program were instead used to teach teachers how to teach every child to read. How fortunate for first grader Erick that his teacher, Anthony Griffin, knew how to help all of the students in his class learn to read. Anthony ensures no child is left behind.

Teaching Him to Read

Anthony John Vincent Griffin

I taught Erick's older siblings; he's the third of four children. The two eldest learned English so they could translate for their Spanish-speaking mother. I remember Erick's sister smiling through tears when I read the book, *I Speak English for My Mom*. Erick's motivation came from sibling rivalry, activated when his brother taunted, "He can't read." Erick had spent his first year of school with an untrained beginning teacher in a haphazard, make-shift combination K–1 class, lost and unchallenged among peers who either lacked social skills or had learning disabilities. Early in first grade it became evident that Erick couldn't spell his last name or use a pair of scissors. Erick claimed, "The scissors don't work." After I taught him how to get the scissors to work, I wondered how I was going to make reading work for Erick.

Not surprisingly, Erick scored the lowest in the class on a series of 15 entry-level assessments. According to the state, standards to be mastered in kindergarten include name and letter writing and beginning reading. Where to begin with Erick who had mastered neither? As a student of and teacher trained in the whole-language approach who also incorporated systematic, explicit phonics, I have emerged as a research-practitioner. My reading plan is not as prescriptive as it is nurturing, focusing on results. So as a community of learners, Room 12 and Erick set out to answer the scientific question, What Do Good Readers Do?

The year begins with *Oh How I Wished I Could Read*, a funny picture book about a boy who wakes up to discover that he can't read and so endures a series of tribulations, he sits on WET PAINT, a very real consequence of reading failure. Students who understand why reading is important are then ready to discover how to read. We then read *Hey, I'm Reading!*, a picture book by Betty Miles that describes in kid-friendly language how to read. At the start of each lesson I ask students (and subconsciously myself) why are we doing this and I get answers. When a student is reading aloud and gets stuck on a sight word, Erick raises his hands and says, "That's a sight word." The students make connections through class discourse how the reading strategies support the bigger goal of being a good reader. Once Erick and the others begin to understand why we do things, problems diminish and they are more engaged.

Still, as the year progressed, Erick wasn't quite having the success of his classmates. Frustrated when others read aloud, he began to lose his motivation. He stopped looking at the words when we echoed or choral read. He interrupted a read-aloud with, "Can we play with the puppets?" On the first spelling test he correctly spelled 6 out of 10 words, but on the next test he alone scored a zero. Immediate intervention in a small group instruction earned him a round of applause from his classmates and the opportunity to take a bow on our class stage for going up 9 points. Erick had made the connection between strategies and success.

By late October, with the help of his older brother, Erick learned all of the 26 sight words, averaged 58% on weekly spelling tests, and although he wasn't volunteering to read out loud from the decodable books, he eagerly volunteered to read the familiar text in daily math assignments. Erick enjoyed the class-authored books the most, making the connection between print and writing. Students acted out and recited their pages from *Holiday ABC* (e.g., "K is for Kwanzaa. Let's light the kinara"), allowing Erick to make yet another connection: visualizing is making a book come to life.

A community walk took us all to the public library and led to our participation in Paws to Read, an exceptionally unique family literacy program that uses rescued dogs, rabbits, and guinea pigs trained as reading partners for children. The hypothesis is that by reading to their nonjudgmental and attentive furry companions, children (especially English-language learners) are able to improve their reading skills. One evening a month, participating students and teachers engage in literacy-related activities, and the following Saturday the children read to a dog, rabbit, or guinea pig on Dog Day Afternoons. Erick enthusiastically chose books beyond his independent reading level and asked to practice with me. The program has improved Erick's confidence. The smile on his face stretched from ear to ear when he first read 132 words in a minute, more than anyone else. That earned him another round of applause and another bow on our class stage; a Kodak moment forever framed in my teaching soul. After 18 weeks, Eric's reading fluency was in the 75th percentile. I know Erick will continue to take bows on our class stage, and I hope I've also prepared him to stand on a much bigger stage, be it at a graduation ceremony or on the center stage in his own lifelong pursuit as he continues learning.

Accomplished teachers teach children first and then they teach curriculum. They find ways to reach every child and to make learning relevant and meaningful by engaging students in their own lives and building from there. They create classrooms where it's safe to risk stretching yourself, even when the goal appears out of reach. Their classrooms are coffeehouses and libraries, and they mirror free-enterprise systems. Older children publish books for younger students. Teachers push their students out and beyond the classroom door through contests and other publishing ventures.

Great teachers are continuously learning along with their students. There is no finished teacher, one who knows it all and has all the answers. The art and craft of teaching is continuously evolving. Each student presents a unique challenge. Content changes as the world shrinks and information grows simultaneously. Teachers know the subjects they teach and how to teach those subjects so students can learn.

REFLECTION

1. What are the essential understandings, the big ideas you want students to take away from your class? Why are these important and meaningful? In what ways are they relevant for students now? How will they be relevant in 5 years? In 10 years?

2. Think about some of your experiences in school. What big ideas have you retained? What did you learn that remains important and meaningful?

3. How do the essential understandings you have retained match or mismatch with those you want for your students? Why is this important?

RESOURCES

If you can read only one book, choose the following:

Wiggins, G., & McTighe, J. (1998). *Understanding by design.* Alexandria, VA: Association for Supervision and Curriculum Development.

Other worthwhile books include the following:

Erickson, H. L. (2001). *Stirring the head, heart, and soul: Redefining curriculum and instruction* (2nd ed.). Thousand Oaks, CA: Corwin Press.

Hull, G., & Schultz, K. (Eds). (2002). *School's out! Bridging out-of-school literacies with classroom practice.* New York: Teachers College Press.

Lambert, L., Walker, D., Zimmerman, D. P., Cooper, J. E., Lambert, M. D., Gardner, M. E., & Szabo, M. (2002). *The constructivist leader* (2nd ed.). Oxford, OH: National Staff Development Council.

Marzano, R. J., Pickering, D. J., & Pollock, J. E. (2000). *Classroom instruction that works: Research-based strategies for increasing student achievement.* Alexandria, VA: Association for Supervision and Curriculum Development.

REFERENCES

Lee, J. O. (2003). Implementing high standards in urban schools: Problems and solutions. *Phi Delta Kappan 84*(6), 449–455.

Ohanian, S. (1999). *One size fits few: The folly of educational standards.* Portsmouth, NH: Heinemann.

Reeves, D. B. (2001). *Making standards work: How to implement standards-based assessments in the classroom, school, and district.* Denver, CO: Advanced Learning Centers.

Reeves, D. B. (2002). *The leader's guide to standards: A blueprint for educational equity and excellence.* San Francisco: Jossey-Bass.

Schwartz, P. (1996). *The art of the long view: Planning for the future in an uncertain world.* New York: Currency-Doubleday.

Teachers Are Responsible for Managing and Monitoring Student Learning

We assess what our students can do, we determine which strategies will help them to continue their academic growth. We reassess and we select in a never-ending chain until the year ends, and then we begin with a new group of students. Some students are so resistant to our efforts we're tempted to quit rather than fight. Teaching is hard work; the general consensus is that it takes 5 to 8 years to learn the art and craft of teaching. Learning isn't always fun either. There are things we ask of our students that aren't fun but that are the necessary building blocks for further accomplishment. Learning is continuous. Think about what you can teach your students now that they will need to know in 20 years. Teach them to learn, to seek understanding, to ask their own questions and find their own answers. Empower your students. Empower yourself to use your student work to inform your own teaching. Along the way of teaching and learning sometimes something magical happens and we know just what to say and what to do and it works. Resistance disappears and learning begins.

Role Model

Alfee Enciso

The ninth-grade girl sitting at her desk was overweight, lazy, and brilliant, but her attitude and defiant behavior sent me into a paroxysm of teacher frustration.

Only 3 minutes into a free writing assignment for my freshman English class and Karla had already stopped writing. While other students wrote furiously about anything they wanted during the initial writer's workshop, Karla sat glumly in her chair picking at her pen and staring off into space. When I peered over her desk to see what she had written, I saw only one sentence: My community is full of sex and violence. Anticipating my concern, she blurted, "I'm done!" and then glared at me like, "Go ahead and try and make me write more. You said I could write anything I wanted. Well, I did, and I'm done."

What I sensed in her writer's block and recalcitrant mood was a reflection of her environment. Like many of the kids I teach in Los Angeles, Karla did live in a violent, dysfunctional community that teased even children from caring parents and strong community roots into a deceptively cruel mirage of a gang lifestyle and steamy sexuality that promised excitement from the pangs of racism, poverty, and boredom the inner city often suffers from.

Luckily, on this day, I had the words and wisdom of Nancy Atwell and Barry Lane to fall back on before my father's impatient temper or my own mother's caustic judgment would get the best of me and destroy what little confidence Karla hung onto as a student. Using a revision method Lane calls *assaulting with questions*, I sat next to Karla, excitement in my eyes, an actor in my soul, and exclaimed, "Wow, you live there too? So do I!"

Karla looked at me like I was crazy. Why was this man she barely knew talking about where he lived—"The rollin' 60s"—and making jokes about the drunks that be digging up his trash cans? She probably thought her acting out would get her negative attention, but instead, she was being praised for writing only one sentence and getting too much information on her garrulous teacher's personal life.

"Sex, really? What kind? Who? What kind of violence have you seen? Karla, I want to know more."

And then I lied, "Karla, you have something here, this could be published."

Okay, my stretches of hyperbole are legendary among my students and colleagues, but even I have limits on the amount of balderdash I can dish out. Guilt ridden, I quickly added, "But you have to show, not tell. Karla, your experiences and writing are important. You've got to go into much more detail."

While the rest of the class quietly wrote their stories, Karla and I whispered to one another like two kids at a sleepover about all the drama on our respective blocks in the Crenshaw corridor. Each story we shared seemed to top the previous one recounted. When the bell rang, Karla promised she'd have a first draft by the next day. A broad smile beamed across her face as she bounced out to lunch.

Four weeks, three revisions, and two writer's conferences later, I read to my fourth-period English class a story from the local forum section of the newspaper about their community. Karla wasn't paying close attention when I began reading aloud, but when I got to the part that said, "I looked outside and there I saw her on the ground bleeding to death. I started to cry even harder. I held her in my hands and told her it would be OK. I called my mother and told her to call the police. She called immediately. She got shot in the shoulder. I'm so glad she is OK now. She moved away quickly from this madness. Me, I'm still in the 'hood hanging on strong, though," she realized the words I mouthed were hers.

After I read her essay and the author's name, the class clapped, and again, Karla's cherubic cheeks widened and let the sunshine of her smile brighten the room. Karla wasn't the only one who was proud of her publication. The next week I happened to bump into her mom and her proud smile was still pasted on her. She thanked me profusely and assured me that she had plenty of copies of the newspaper article. It was only March, but for me, the school year could have ended in April.

Since I taught only ninth graders at Dorsey, I didn't see much of Karla or any of my students from '99. Every once in a while I would spy Karla in the spring during the softball season (my classroom bungalow presses against the right-field fence of the school's baseball diamond) or around campus during an assembly, but for the most part, my energies and attention were focused on my present-day classes and the new scrubs that filled my room.

From time to time I still think of Karla and the other students that I've reached, but the years and polyglot of students I've taught clot my mind like the dust and debris that seeps into my room from the playing fields close by. And while I knew that Karla graduated and was going on to college, I just didn't know where, or when, or how. In the busy end-of-the-year responsibilities, I missed her graduation.

During the summers (and now winters and springs) I spend a vast amount of time at UCLA, my second educational home and professional development mecca (I'm a UCLA Writing Project fellow). On those lazy Saturday mornings, I fork over seven dollars to one of the college students at the parking kiosk, then drive to the parking structure and give my paid-for ticket to another student who then sticks the printed pass inside my car's windshield before I'm free to park.

Normally, I'm on autopilot when going through these vehicular motions, but the sight of Karla doling out tickets at the entrance of the garage stopped me in the middle of my traffic lane and forced me to get out my car. Horns honked, but I didn't care. Each step I took erased months of time. Four years turned into just last week and the young college coed handing out tickets in the front of the line finally noticed me.

It was my Karla: happy, smiling Karla, still strong, still thriving, and very much the role model of her 'hood. We hugged and both smiled one of her big Kool-Aid grins and then parted to our commitments, leaving words for another day.

One up, hundreds to follow.

There is much we can do as teachers to help our students be successful. However, we need to remember that we're not the only ones in the classroom. They aren't empty vessels into which we pour the knowledge we have. Learning requires active engagement, not quiet seat time. Several of our area middle schools have been examining their students' test scores and analyzing them compared with the grades students earn in class. Big surprise! Very low test scores are often matched with very high grades. We pass the students along to high school where teachers expect students to learn the assigned material. It's not sufficient to be a nice kid, get along with others, and have good attendance. Teachers are responsible for monitoring what the students are learning, not for making subjective judgments. And students are equally responsible for their learning. Their classmates often play a role.

One Meeting You Won't Mind Attending

Patrice J. Faison

At the beginning of each school year we work on developing a classroom learning community whose foundation is respect. Respect is both given and expected—from student to student, student to teacher, and teacher to student. This concept of classroom community is not easy for some students since many are not used to having a say in how their classroom works, how things will be taught, and what materials should be used. To help establish our classroom community we conduct weekly class meetings, more often if needed. During the class meetings we sit in a circle and discuss classroom issues. For example, if there's a problem with homework being turned in, we address ways to solve the problem. By involving students in the solution, problems diminish.

Tonya was a quiet third grader in my class who was constantly tardy or absent. Tonya's mother was a single mother trying hard to provide for her daughter and herself. Her mother thought Tonya didn't want to come to school because she didn't like school. It was months into the school year, without improvement in Tonya's behavior, before Tonya's mother confided that Tonya had no school friends, that no one in class liked her. I found this difficult to believe because Tonya was such a sweet girl.

For the next 3 days I observed Tonya during the academic day and during recess. I noticed that she didn't mingle or converse with many students. I called a class meeting during which we addressed the issues of friendship and making new friends. Although I carefully avoided calling attention to any child by name, Tonya opened up and stated how she felt. The students quickly rallied around Tonya and made her feel a part of the class. Over the next weeks she played well with others and developed a close best friend. I realized the importance of our class meetings and what a classroom community really meant. The decrease in Tonya's tardies and absences was dramatic. Her mother reported a change in her attitude toward school. Needless to say, we continued with our class meetings and our classroom community continued to prosper.

Although teachers have a responsibility to monitor and assess student progress in their classes, our role doesn't end there. It's important that we also monitor the district, state, and federal tests and surveys our students are required to take. One inquiring mind, David Feela, taught me a few things about how some tests and surveys are put together. In this case David and I are the learners, and you will be also. One of the lessons I learned from David's story is that it is important that any assessment tool we use, formal or informal, formative or summative, be meaningful. Assessments should help teachers and students know what has been mastered and what needs to come next. They shouldn't be games without meaning. You be the judge on this one.

A Gram of Truth

David Feela

While the students darkened the bubbles on the survey forms with their No. 2 lead pencils, I sat in my chair at the front of the classroom and surveyed the class. They had been assigned the task of completing a drug questionnaire, an annual statistical portrait of our youth that provides funding for our school district's Student Assistance Program. They groaned when I distributed the booklets, but they went right to work, relieved to know that I had no interest in reading their answers. My instructions, to ensure confidentiality, required that I leave a large manila envelope in the open so students could place their completed surveys inside it; the last student finished was to seal the results.

Ten minutes into the survey, one student's hand shot into the air. "Yes?" I responded. "What's Derbisol?" the student inquired. I had no idea. The entire class glanced up from its paperwork, looking to me for guidance. I asked for the page number the student was working on and picked up an extra copy of the survey. The item in question read, "Have you ever used Derbisol?" Then it asked, "How often?" This was a drug I knew nothing about. "Sorry," I said, "I can't help you on this one but if you ever find out, I'd like to know." The student smiled and continued filling in the bubbles.

After all the surveys were safely tucked away in the manila envelope, I thought I might try for closure and add a little meaning to the thankless task of filling out surveys by asking my students to air some of their feelings about drugs. "So, what percentage of your fellow students would you guess use drugs?" I asked, trying to avoid the tone of an impersonal statistician who seeks data by masking any interest in anyone's experience. A few dispassionate faces broke into grins at the back of the room, as if I had just asked what color they thought the sky might be on a clear, cloudless day.

"A lot!" one student replied. "A lot? How much is a lot? 50%? 60%? 80%?" The faces turned passive again. I had made the mistake of quoting numbers. Quickly, I decided on another approach. "If you wanted to get your hands on some drugs, how difficult would it be?"

I immediately sensed I had made another mistake, like I'd been trying to put the finger on one of their friends while working as a part-time undercover narcotics officer. Even the trust offered in simple eye contact was withdrawn. I, too, glanced down at my hands and seriously considered returning to a discussion of our novel. There they could rely on me getting involved with the problems of fictional characters and staying clear of their lives, all in smooth accordance with the inclusion of Standard 6 in my lesson plan, the one that mandates, *Students read and recognize literature as a record of human experience.* But then a young lady who continued staring out the window said in a matter-of-fact voice, "Around the corner you can get anything you want." "Really?" I asked in astonishment. "Really," she echoed, and a half dozen other students nodded agreement, like ripples moving away from a pebble that had just been tossed into a pond.

I finished the day with this new drug, Derbisol, stuck in my thoughts. Apparently, enough young people came in contact with such a substance—perhaps even on a daily basis—to include it on a major survey. While I knew everything I needed to know about Shakespeare,

Hemingway, and Hardy, I had no idea where Derbisol crept into the cultural picture. In all likelihood I had unwittingly crossed that danger-ous line called middle age and begun my inevitable trot toward the shady lane that leads out to the pasture. Derbisol? It sounded like it had the makings of a big-time pharmaceutical, a prescription drug gone under the counter.

The next day I stopped by to pick the brain of our resident health expert, a man who, if he hadn't heard something about it, at least knew how to find out. Unfortunately, he had no more idea than I did, but having taken the opportunity to ask one of his students who appeared to know his science he guessed that Derbisol served as an ingredient in many VCR and computer cleaning solutions. "Ah," I said, "then it works like an inhalant?" He carefully sucked in his breath: "Perhaps."

The next day while working in the library with my class, I headed for the spot where the medical reference books are shelved. I pulled a few volumes down, flipped to the index, and scanned for the word Derbisol. Once again, the drug eluded me. I went over to the dictionary, the one that might give me a hernia if I were to lift it off its pedestal. Still, no Derbisol. I was beginning to suspect Derbisol of being a hallu-cinogen, one that vanished without any trace when the authorities started looking for it. The librarian noticed my puzzled expression and asked if she could help. I told her about my drug problem, wondered if Derbisol could be a nickname, like Lucy In the Sky With Diamonds. She promised to check the Internet.

Later she handed me a copy of an article. "So, how do they take the stuff?" I queried. "They take it with a grain of salt," was all that she'd say. It seems that in designing drug surveys, writers often include an item or two to check the reliability of their respondents' answers. The writ-ers invent drugs like Derbisol. The drug is a fake; the survey writers made it up. But in some surveys, results indicated that as many as 5.6% of the respondents report using these nonexistent drugs. Clearly, here's an awkward high, especially when compared to the slim 3.6% who report using heroin. That makes Derbisol a far more popular drug because, well, mainly it's cheaper.

I know that parents all across this country worry about the kind of influences their children will encounter when they enter the public schools, especially the high schools. Here's abiding proof for me that one overwhelming influence is still as prevalent today as it was back when I went to school: the desire to appear no different from anyone else. It's not that drug abuse is not a problem to take seriously, but when I see a student raise his or her hand in the future and ask, "What is Derbisol?" I'm just going to say, "It's worse than heroin" and that's the truth.

Teachers are human. There are times when they want to toss a student aside and say, enough is enough. Some do just that, but most of us don't. We just dig a little deeper into our repertoire and figure out another approach that just may work. The teachers who remain in education are among the world's greatest optimists. We really believe we can reach every student; and if we can't, it won't be from lack of trying.

"Fair Is Foul, and Foul Is Fair"

Joel Kammer

After three disciplinary run-ins in as many weeks with Eric, a student in my regular 12th grade English class (nonacademic, non-college prep), I was ready to write the final referral that would get him expelled, out of my class and out of my life. Tempting as that sounded, I was not yet quite ready to give up on him. I knew this about him: though he was classified as a high school senior he had never attended a high school before. He had been homeschooled and then shuttled through a variety of alternative programs during the past few years. He lived with an uncle who tried to control Eric's behavior, but wasn't successful. My class was Eric's final stop. He was on a strict behavioral and academic contract and he either had to get control of his antisocial behavior or be out of school permanently. I wasn't ready to be the one to make the decision that might negatively affect him for the rest of his life.

I teach and also work part-time as a beginning teacher support provider. Our school is crowded, so I'm one of the traveling teachers who move from room to room. Eric's class met in a room that another teacher had had to himself for several years. It was a disheveled, cramped, dark, and uninviting place filled with odd memorabilia: 1970s newspapers, dozens of chessboards, and an African drum. With three weeks left before beginning a semester-ending poetry unit, I decided on a whirlwind tour of *Macbeth*. A little Shakespeare couldn't hurt. At that point in early November, Eric's grade hovered between 30% and 40%, a solid F.

For a first assignment, I asked students to draw what they wanted the audience to see as the curtains opened for their own production of Macbeth. All they knew was that the play featured three witches on a Scottish heath. They brought their artwork to the next class. Some were carefully rendered and took into consideration such elements as colorful backgrounds, dry-ice ground fog, steaming cauldrons, and elaborate costuming. Eric's hurriedly penciled version featured three small stick figures with conical witch hats and sketchy brooms floating in the middle of an otherwise blank page. Students explained their choices and how they had taken my bare-bones instructions in a given direction. Predictably, Eric had little to say, other than making a few witch jokes.

To begin reading the play I divided the class into four groups, one for each of the three witches and one for the weather. The weather group, which included Eric and his friend Enrique, a Brazilian exchange student who loves reggae music, worked on orchestrating thunder and lightning for the background. We did a run-through of the one-page Act 1 Scene 1 and, not surprisingly, it was awful. But it was awful in a funny way and students offered several suggestions for improvement. For a few minutes, class was chaotic, students shouting out ideas, arguing over procedures. Then, amazingly, Eric took over. He appointed one of his group members to work the light switch for simulated lightning flashes. He moved the witch groups to various parts of the room for effect. He had everyone practicing fist pounding on tables and foot stamping on the floor to produce effectively staged rolls of pseudo-thunder that moved across the room. After a few more practice attempts during which Eric gave directions and encouragement, he asked me whether he could use the African drum resting in the corner. I reluctantly gave permission and he brought it into the center of the room where he stationed himself and Enrique to either side. He signaled for quiet, then cued the light-switch operator, counted silently to three, signaled the thunder, and then each of the witches in turn, all the while adding drum rolls to each burst of thunder. By the time the whole class shouted in unison, "Fair is foul, and foul is fair," everyone was smiling or laughing (though not missing cues), and on his signal to cut to the last roll of thunder, we heard a burst of applause from the classroom on one side of us and an answering roll of foot-stamping thunder from the class on the other side. Before he left that day Eric thanked me for allowing him to use the drum.

Continuing through *Macbeth* Eric volunteered to read aloud (badly but with determination), commented on the portions of film we watched (especially the scenes involving the witches), and completed all assigned work. During the poetry unit that followed he continued in the same positive vein. He commented on other students' poetry; he made an attempt to analyze poems. He read his own work aloud, sometimes to the accompaniment of Enrique's drumming. He passed the fall semester with a marginal grade and is still in school as of this writing. He's still not likely to graduate on time, but he's showing up for every class and making an effort on virtually every assignment.

In the greater scheme of things, his Shakespearean directorial experience may have little effect on his life; he still has lots of problems and still faces daunting challenges. He has, however, had a taste of academic achievement, of leading his peers in a positive direction, of working hard to reach a goal—passing English. Passing English may have little practical use for him and will never show up on any report of test scores, but it just might have deposited a permanent taste for how good learning and participation can feel.

There is a wealth to be found in the heterogeneous classroom. I've rarely encountered a child who, given the opportunity, didn't have something to offer to the class. That I have had any students I thought didn't have something to offer is really an indictment of myself as a teacher, much more so than it is about the students. When teachers have a mind-set that every child can learn, that each offers something unique, they do. Yolanda was a quiet middle schooler, identified by her low academic skills, but her intelligence was there, waiting for the right opportunity. She was fortunate to find teacher Cindy Taylor.

A Gift of Progress

Cindy Taylor

Providing students opportunities to blossom is important. Middle school students especially are on a journey of personal discovery. As an English teacher I believe one of my responsibilities is to foster the positive attributes that will help them in this process. By selecting relevant young adult literature, students have multiple models and opportunities to strengthen their personal development. Yolanda, who began as an extremely quiet eighth grader, is one of my most memorable successes.

Yolanda rarely volunteered and did not interact much with her peers in class, at lunch, or after school. When she did speak, her voice was so soft that it was difficult to hear her. Yolanda worked with others in groups, but for the most part she remained quiet. She could easily get lost working with more talkative students. I think she compensated for her low reading and writing skills through shyness. Over the course of the year Yolanda frequently talked with me after school while she waited for her ride home. She asked questions about assignments, but only one-on-one, never in front of the class. Through her journal writings I learned about her and her family, so there was a lot for us to talk about.

Reading Lois Lowry's *The Giver* was the breakthrough for Yolanda. Its final resolution is open to interpretation, much to the dismay of many readers. When Jonas's story ended, my students wanted to go beyond the book's ending. I decided to let them work through their own ideas first and then to explore their ideas in groups. I mixed struggling and proficient readers, talkative and reticent students. I promised to share what the author thought the extended solution would be.

On the morning of the group assignment, Yolanda asked, "Are we finally going to find out what happened?" Imagine my surprise at hearing her ask a question in front of the class. "Yes," I replied, "Right after the groups present their opinions." The students were eager to share their ideas. I circulated around the room stopping to listen to their discussions. Yolanda's group had some very eager readers in it. These students were the vocal ones who were not easily swayed by other opinions. Yolanda's careful reading of the text's clues led her to have a very different opinion from the other students. At a pause in the conversation, she spoke. Her quiet voice told the others that she saw things differently. She carefully explained her reasons and justified her conclusions. The others listened, but they didn't change their minds. Nevertheless, I was proud of her for speaking out.

We reassembled as a whole class and I showed the author's Web site with her concept of what happened to the main character after the book. Yolanda's face beamed when the class learned that her theory coincided with the author's. She had picked up on some clues that the other, more vocal students had overlooked. When we complimented her on her analysis her smile grew wider.

After that, Yolanda's confidence in her reading skills, and in her social skills, improved. It was a small victory for me, her teacher, but it was a significant one for Yolanda. Teachers receive many gifts. Yolanda is one that I'll treasure.

When I was a child, all the students who had exceptional needs, who were physically challenged, went elsewhere, not to the public schools where I went. I spent 12 years in public school without ever thinking about kids in wheelchairs or who were blind or deaf; there simply weren't any. Now I have a granddaughter who has physical challenges and I am grateful every day that she is mainstreamed, that her classmates include her in their games. Everyone has a richer experience because the children are together; there's diversity, not only of color and religion, but of abilities as well. Schools that are inclusive, that don't segregate, are representative of what democracy can be. These schools, and the children in them, should be treated like the treasures they are. Sometimes gifts arrive in the form of cookies wrapped in newspapers; other times they are measures of student progress. Perhaps the most valuable gifts we receive as teachers are the lessons we learn from our students while we are teaching them.

A Lesson About Diversity From Kyle

Linda T. Johnson

Every day I try to teach in ways that inspire, motivate, and transmit a love for learning to my first-grade students. I also want my students to develop a sense of self-worth, so I acknowledge and accept differences and appreciate the ways their differences add richness to our class. Luckily for me, every so often a child comes along and challenges me in ways to guarantee that I continue to remain child-focused. This year Kyle, a child with numerous physical problems, presented my greatest challenge and taught me the most.

Kyle and his mother attended the Meet the Teacher Day prior to the beginning of school, and with the saddest eyes, his mom pleaded with me to "just give him a chance." She was well aware that I knew from Kyle's student files that documentation was in place for Kyle to be placed in Special Education classes in a nearby school. If, after 6 weeks, I concurred with the recommendations, Kyle would no longer be a candidate for inclusion within the regular classroom.

I looked at Kyle with his thick eyeglasses, dual hearing aids, and small body. Reluctantly I understood how it might be easy to make assumptions about this child based on his physical appearance. Then he smiled at me and I was hopelessly in love. I told his mom I would work with her as the kind of teacher I would want for my own children.

My classroom communicates my belief that learning is a social experience because I know that the connection between social competence and academic success is of critical importance since *how* children learn is as important as *what* children learn. Therefore, often the greatest academic growth comes through social interaction. I provided Kyle an alternative to worksheets through a balanced literacy approach in reading and Language Arts. The curriculum supported Kyle's imagination, creativity, and curiosity. We explored art, music, and drama. We handled manipulatives in Math class, read and wrote in Language Arts, became scientists, and applied the social studies disciplines. Throughout the day, while Kyle participated in activities and centers, I kept extensive anecdotal records. Assessment and evaluation revealed not only Kyle's preferred learning methods, strengths, and needs, but also that his knowledge base was greater than previously thought. The gaps in learning were not as significant. While the days turned into weeks, I noticed that Kyle possessed an abundance of common sense, was developing a dry sense of humor, and always had an answer for higher level thinking questions. He frequently amazed me. Kyle needed certain modifications due to problems with his large and small motor coordination, as well as his hearing and sight difficulties. But he made it clear from the first few weeks that he didn't want to be considered different in any way.

I will never forget the day that Kyle read to me for the first time. I cried. That night, when he read to his mother, she cried, and the next day at school, we cried together. I am helping Kyle's mother in her fight to keep Kyle from being incorrectly identified for self-contained Special Education classes. In addition, as a tribute to Kyle, I recently wrote a teaching tolerance grant that is providing a program with materials for the K–2 teachers and students in my school to help make all of us more aware of the dangers of judging others based on physical appearances. Just when I thought I knew a great deal, there came Kyle to teach me even more.

In spite of all of the research that points to the negative effects of early retention, we still do it. By what criteria are children retained and to what end? Repeating the same things, taught the same ways, is not likely to get anything but the same results. One teacher labels a child a failure while another finds the hook to move the child along. How many students are housed in self-contained Special Education classes when they could be mainstreamed like Kyle? How many of our children are retained due to the combined failure of the teacher and school to monitor and intervene in a timely manner? There isn't enough information in the story that follows to know why José was retained in second grade, but there is enough to know why he'd be successful from now on.

José

David Ross

José was showing signs that would worry any teacher. He'd been retained in second grade and because he was big for his age, he looked like a fourth grader sitting among small third graders. He knew he looked out of place and felt it. He was often frustrated and frequently gave up on an assignment within minutes after beginning. Then he'd announce to the class, "I don't care anyway." A bad divorce left him with no father in his life and a mother who showed little interest. He didn't feel valued at school or at home. José had more challenges than anyone whose age was measured by a single digit should have. Somehow I needed to help José to be successful and proud of himself.

One day I was reading aloud to my class the book *Captain Underpants* by Dave Pilkey. The entire class, especially José, took a great interest in the comical story. For the first time I saw a light igniting in his eyes. Following the reading, I asked, "Would you be interested in reading more books by the same author?" He nearly shouted, "Yes!" The next day in the library I showed him how he could locate authors. He didn't take long to figure out how to do it. His feet might have begun by walking the short trip to the fiction shelves, but he ended up sprinting to the books by his new favorite author. He thumbed through the various titles with anticipation and was delighted with what he found. Temporary disappointment followed because there's a two-book limit on checkouts. He took his two, determined to return for the rest.

Over the course of the next few weeks he eventually managed to check out and read six chapter books by Pilkey. I know he read them cover to cover because he knew the plots along with details and characters of every story. He became well versed in the adventures of Captain Underpants. He even purchased some of his own editions at a school book sale. His enthusiasm for these books was contagious. I began seeing them in the hands of most of the other students in our class. I often heard them discussing the stories. Many, including José, chose to read during lunch and recess instead of playing on the yard. He had started a trend and his face showed his excitement.

Even after he read all of the available books, I was happy to see that a passion kept burning within José. He had an idea to write his own stories based on the characters he had been reading about. I encouraged him to be an author, but cautioned him to create his own stories and not copy an existing one. He agreed. I provided the supplies he needed and he couldn't wait to get started.

After writing, illustrating, editing, and revising, all on his own clock, he finished his first book. At this point he needed no more encouragement as there was no stopping him. He asked me to make multiple copies of his book so he could sell them. I, of course, agreed to be his publisher. Before I was done copying his book he had already created a sign advertising his books for sale—"25 cents a copy." I allowed him to post it in the classroom. He sold out the first edition.

I proudly helped him to publish two more stories that he co-wrote with a friend. His classmates purchased all of the copies. He motivated other students to write their own books as well. It's hard to believe that he had needed to be retained; maybe he only needed to be inspired. Thanks to Captain Underpants and the world of books he opened up, I know that José is going to be OK.

In its simplest form our job as teachers is to feed students academic knowledge so they can negotiate the world they live in. But sometimes, before we can expose them to Shakespeare or the Pythagorean theorem, we have to feed them lunch; we have to touch them and show them we care.

Hunger

Shelia Sutton

When I met Danny, I knew from his bright smile and keen sense of humor that he had spunk. Soon after that I also knew that Danny had difficulty sitting still, that he was not interested in schoolwork, and that he had a history of academic failure. But even so his smile lit up the room each time he entered. His humor, which often bordered on silliness, was so contagious that he quickly developed a reputation for being a distraction to his classmates who were, in fact, in freshman English to learn. After weeks spent trying unsuccessfully to motivate Danny to put his enthusiasm and high levels of energy to work for him academically, I was ready to give up. I had modified the instruction. I had moved his seat, set strict boundaries for his behavior, and done everything I had learned in my 13 years of teaching. Nothing seemed to be working. My enjoyment of him was becoming clouded by my feelings of despair. Danny was totally disconnected and was beginning to willfully act out against me and my efforts to engage him academically. We were at an impasse.

And, then, I wrote him a note on a Post-it pad that truthfully said, "I'm concerned about you, but I'm not sure what role I should play in this. I really care about you and want to help. What do you think would be most useful for me to do or not to do? What do you see as the problem?" I handed it to him and walked away. After a few moments, Danny called me aside and said, "I'm hungry all of the time." I was astonished. I didn't know what to say. Danny was in my fifth period class, which met just after lunch. Before I said anything to him, I walked over to my desk, pulled out $1.50, and sent him to the cafeteria to get lunch. When he returned, and the rest of his classmates were busy working in groups, Danny and I had a conversation that helped me to get to know him and understand his situation on a deeper level. It was a life-changing encounter for both of us.

I discovered that Danny's mom is a recovering crack addict, that Danny is a crack baby, and that social service is already involved with helping the family. Even so, Danny's basic needs were still not being met sufficiently. He said he had been afraid of telling anyone since he believed his mom was trying, in spite of her repeated and recent relapses. If I hadn't asked him what the problem was, I'm convinced he'd have never confided in me.

After Danny and I took care of his hunger pangs, we spent the next few days negotiating how he would spend the rest of his time in my classroom. We decided that his assignments would be discussed, modified, and agreed upon daily and that he would be held accountable by me and by his classmates for his academic performance. I typed out his assignments onto 2-inch strips of paper and handed them to him as he entered the class each day. Sometimes the assignments called for him to work alone and at other times it called for him to engage one or more of his classmates. Each assignment required that he meet with proficiency the state standards we were addressing in class. Soon Danny began to take ownership of his learning. I could see that he looked forward to coming to class and that he felt a deep sense of belonging. His sense of self blossomed and he began to use his humor and bright smile to encourage his classmates to get their work done. He no longer distracted them, but rather called them to account. Danny worked hard to meet the academic standards, and in June he had moved from a *far below basic* performance to a *basic* performance in several of the power standards our class had spent the year focusing on.

When I asked Danny what it was that had made the difference for him, he replied, "When you gave me money for lunch I knew that you cared about me. No teacher has ever done anything like that before. It made me want to do better." Danny is now a sophomore and he visits every week. We talk about his continued struggle and his persistent progress, and I let him know how proud I am of his new hunger—for learning.

Just as many of you know when that special child walks into your room, a child who will get under your skin, who will teach you something you need to learn at that point in time, so it is with me. I teach teachers and meet hundreds of wonderful teachers every year. But each year, one or two or three stay with me. Jay Schwartz is one of those teachers. I first spent time with her when she arranged a meeting with her new superintendent and a few other teachers. She had gotten the superintendent's attention by writing him a letter about the National Board and the possibilities it held for improving student achievement in the district. The superintendent listened and Jay talked. She told him about what she had already learned since she'd begun working on her National Board portfolio two months before. I also listened. Jay was questioning everything she had done up to that time in her classes teaching the severely disabled. She was hungry to do more, to reach children she hadn't reached before. One of the portfolio entries for the Exceptional Needs Specialist certificate requires the candidate to assess his or her students' needs, pose a question about what it would be like if . . . , and then proceed to answer it. That assignment changed the way Jay saw her students and will forever see her students. I thought her reflection was one of the most powerful I have ever read. Herein lies the power of truly seeing our students and not resting until we add value to every one.

Finding Freddie

Macre Jay Schwartz

Each year eight new students with exceptional challenges come to my kindergarten classroom. Mine is a class for students with severe cognitive and physical disabilities. Even among all of the other severely challenged children, Freddie stood out to me almost immediately. His diagnosis of autism meant that he had deficits in socialization and communication, and as soon as I met him I knew he was going to be my biggest challenge of the year.

Freddie was not able to participate in our classroom activities and was often isolated from the group. Sometimes that was his choice, and often it was because he was too disruptive to be with the rest of the class. Freddie spent most of his time walking, running, or skipping around the room in circles; he often followed a pattern in the floor. He stood on top of the toys, the chairs, the tables, and even on people. He enjoyed musical toys with lights, but mostly threw them, running and laughing with delight when I came to attend to the crash. Freddie held his breath or gulped air and made loud noises. Sometimes he hit his head and hit others for no apparent reason. Freddie never made any attempt to interact with others and his behavior further isolated him from the group. Students ran away or otherwise avoided him as he came inadvertently close to them. After several unsuccessful attempts I was beginning to think I was not going to have any impact on Freddie. I just could not reach him.

When assessment time came I knew traditional assessment was not going to be effective for Freddie. I spend the assessment time observing his play and trying to discover something, anything, I could go on. After several days I noticed something I hadn't seen initially. Freddie would sit by himself and toss a toy in the air for 5–10 minutes at a time. If he could pay attention to tossing the toy, why couldn't he do so with me for a few minutes? I needed to learn more. I sought help from colleagues and found an assessment tool that might help me to get more answers. The results from the assessment led me to a specialized teaching technique for children with autism. I read all I could find on it and attended a 2-day conference. I learned that I needed to change my whole approach to Freddie. Armed with renewed enthusiasm and a new trick up my sleeve I was ready to find Freddie.

The next day during playtime I sat on the floor next to Freddie as he was tossing a car in the air and watching it fall. As it dropped, I snatched it away. At first Freddie didn't seem to notice, but after a while I seemed to be an irritant. At least he was aware of my presence. My persistence paid off when Freddie threw the car back to me that I had rolled to him. Next I rolled the car on his leg. He looked up at me and smiled. Our interaction lasted only a few minutes, but it was the beginning of a relationship.

My work with Freddie helped me move my focus from my teaching to my students' learning, a monumental change. Those beginning results I had with Freddie, and the work I was able to do with him for the rest of the year, have given me confidence. I'm encouraged to persevere when working with even more challenging students. This made me think about the impact I could have had on students in previous years, the opportunities missed for those kids because I didn't look long enough or hard enough. I learned the real importance of great teaching. I realized that I had been afraid to ask the tough questions about my students' learning because I thought the answers were too difficult to find. I have learned that digging deeper makes instruction more effective and can bring great rewards. I'm now more able to help even the most challenging children find their way to learning.

Jay's persistence, her unwillingness to leave even one child behind, led to her finding the key to bring Freddie, and other severely disabled children, closer to learning. That same unwillingness to settle for mediocrity pushed her to push her superintendent into expecting quality teaching from every teacher in the district. From her beginning as the first homegrown National Board teacher in her district, two dozen more submitted portfolios for assessment and another two dozen teachers have begun the work. We touch one child and we change the world; we touch one teacher and we can change the world. We should never underestimate the power of one.

When teachers first begin considering National Board Certification one of their initial questions inevitably concerns the students they teach. Is there an advantage for teachers with gifted and talented (GATE) identified students? My students are all low, how can I show I'm accomplished? Should I feature my honors class, as their discussions are richer? What about my English Language Learners? Will they hold me back? I assure them, as do other support providers, that the National Board is not pitting one teacher against another. Certification is about demonstrating accomplished teaching, and accomplished teaching comes from adding value to every student who comes into your classroom. That's why it is so critical that we continually monitor what students bring into the classroom with them, what they are learning, and what they still need to master. We've been reminded that we sometimes need to measure achievement and success in inches. And sometimes student achievement is measured in one word.

The Power of Words

Nicki O'Neill

As a speech–language pathologist, some of the children I have on my caseload are nonverbal. Our school has a fairly high population of prekindergarten-age children. Some of them start school as young as 3 years old. Students with developmental delays, speech and language delays, autism, and so on fill our pre-K classrooms. Their classrooms look like any other: little chairs, toys, circle time activities, and the like. The anticipation of meeting their "big school" teacher and making new friends overwhelms these young little beings. On the first day of school they come toddling down the hallway, some with parents in tow, others arrive on the school bus—all ready to start their new adventure. I have always had a special place in my heart for these little ones. Their faces light up with each activity. Their loving hugs and smiles make your day.

Some of my students talk or have learned other ways to communicate at least some of their basic wants and needs. They point, gesture, or throw tantrums to tell you what is going on in their mind. Although I have worked with this population for years, every child touches me in a unique way. When I think that I have hit a brick wall and don't know where to go next to find the strategy to unlock communication, to help the child progress, they always surprise me.

That brings me to Jake. Jake is a 3-year-old little boy who came to our school developmentally delayed and language impaired. He was very attached to mom and did not at first separate easily. Jake was unable to communicate his needs, especially to someone unfamiliar like me. He did not talk at all, made no attempt to imitate vocalizations, and wasn't willing to even play with other children. He began school in the middle of October after one of my pre-K groups had already been formed. The children were well acclimated to the expectations of our therapy sessions. I decided to put Jake with this group of children because they were a little older, they were 4 years old, and had become very verbal by that point. I targeted activities that focused on phonemic awareness and rhyming. I told stories and we sang using props and puppets. The children have access to augmentative forms of communication if they choose to use them. However, verbalizations are always praised the most. Jake came to the group reluctantly. He didn't want to leave the safe haven of his pre-K classroom. Once there he was surrounded and doted on by the other four students. They thought he was cute and wanted to help him. They questioned his unwillingness to talk. This was quite ironic since some of them were just like him a year ago. I explained that everyone was different and that Jake could use an alternate communication strategy to participate with us, just like they had used at one time.

I never force students to participate. Jake began circle time by sitting back beyond the group and observing the rest of us. This was actually fine with me—I knew he was listening to what we were doing. After a few weeks he joined the group, but still verbalized nothing. He was nonverbal in his home environment as well. After a few sessions, I began pairing a verbalization with something motivating—like his favorite toy. Jake soon made the connection and began making some vowel sounds when requesting things he wanted. His vocal repertoire grew quickly; no true words, but something. I was thankful for anything to begin with.

Two months passed, and though Jake was progressing, it was not as quickly as I had hoped for. And then it happened. Jake's mom sent a note telling me that Jake had said his first real word at home, *Mom*. The tone of the letter brought tears. He had never been able to even call his mother before. She reminded me that even the smallest gain, one word, can mean the world.

Elementary art taught by a credentialed art teacher is unfortunately absent from most schools. For those rare elementary schools that are fortunate enough to have an art teacher who works with all of the students, the resulting art lessons can have carry over throughout the curriculum. Sometimes a child is touched by one teacher, sometimes by another. As we've read in some of the previous stories, sometimes it's that most challenging student who teaches us the most and reminds us why we teach. Carley was just such a student, and the lesson Linda Hollett learned from her was the power of a heartfelt compliment.

Carley

Linda Hollett

I'm an elementary art teacher who works on a rotating basis in all of the classrooms at our elementary school. I first meet the students when they are in kindergarten and then watch them grow until they graduate from our fifth grade and move on to the middle school. Carley is one of those students you never forget—you couldn't, even if you tried. She was not an endearing child. She had severe gaps in her learning from moving around a lot and from other problems at home. She couldn't be left in a classroom with other students without adult supervision. She was defiant, sneaky, and a troublemaker, always stirring things up. All through elementary school I battled with her during Art class, sometimes head-to-head. Carley worked halfheartedly, sabotaged her own art work, and disturbed the other students by her outbursts. No matter what I did, there would be nothing but frustration by the end of class.

For more than 2 years I cajoled her, I threatened, I isolated her, and sometimes I just removed her from class completely. Carley's behavior remained the same. I despaired of ever making her behave. And then on a day like any other, at the end of her fourth-grade year, we painted as we had many times before. It was a typical painting assignment: *Paint an underwater scene with fish, show overlapping, texture, some pattern. Use your imagination and don't forget to fill in the background.* We used the usual supplies and materials: tempera paint, easel brushes, 18″ x 24″ paper, and some natural sponges for applying a textured look to the ocean floor, the rocks and caves. My goal was to get Carley through the lesson with as little paint on the floor as possible, and less, if possible, on the other students.

We sketched and then painted. I offered advice and encouragement, pleased with the progress of the students. Everyone was engaged and no one became frustrated or discouraged.

While I cruised around the room I walked by Carley's seat and then stopped dead in my tracks. There she was, focused, attentive, and almost finished with the best piece of artwork in the class. For the first time ever I was filled with admiration. I looked her in the eye, "This is absolutely wonderful." She had created texture with the brush as well as with the sponge. She had arranged her fish and other objects with care. There was sureness in her brushstrokes I had never noticed before. She smiled. I suggested that her painting looked complete and if she agreed she could clean up. That was all. She put the painting on the floor to dry, put her supplies away, and sat down waiting quietly for the other students to finish.

Over the next few weeks Carley completed more art projects. Each time she followed directions and demonstrated an understanding of what she was supposed to be learning. She did her work quickly, efficiently, capably, and without me having to remind her. What had changed? Was this just a fluke? Now she always completed the assignment, always cleaned up without being told, and always did her work with an elegant competence that was inspiring to behold. I smiled at her and she smiled at me—all the time. It had started with that one genuine compliment, one she knew she deserved. I had not forced her to do anything. I had only provided the opportunity for her to learn and to demonstrate what she could do.

I would like to say this turned her life around, but I don't know that. She came by a couple of times in later years and then I lost track of her. I do know that for the rest of that year and for all of her fifth-grade year I looked forward to having her in class. She had become a model student in the Art room, even getting other students to settle down and work. She still had problems in her academic classes. There were still learning gaps, and she still had a difficult home life. But Carley turned my life around.

It was an epiphany, that moment I fully realized the power of a compliment and experienced the amazing effect of a kind word. From that day on I have found ways to build children up, not tear them down. And every time, every time I compliment a child, Carley is there. Thank you, Carley.

When I first read the core proposition—teachers are responsible for managing and monitoring student learning—I could think only about assessments. But managing and monitoring student learning is much greater than giving tests and assigning grades. It's all about choices and pacing and helping students to make connections. It's having a full complement of strategies you can call on as appropriate and colleagues to call upon when you don't have the right strategy, like Jay did when she looked for ways to find Freddie.

In business, effective managers empower their staff to take ownership, to make decisions, to monitor their own work. In classrooms, effective teachers empower their students. Teaching is not something we do to them, teaching and learning is something we do together. In the stories in this chapter we've read about students and teachers, and we've learned that sometimes the lines between the two are blurred—as they should be.

REFLECTION

1. In what ways can I guide students to be the managers and monitors of their own learning? How might these skills impact students' lives?

2. What is the difference between my managing and monitoring student learning and their managing and monitoring their own learning? Why is this an important distinction?

RESOURCES

If you can read only one book, choose the following:
Reeves, D. B. (2001). *Making standards work: How to implement standards-based assessments in the classroom, school, and district.* Denver: Advanced Learning Centers.

Other worthwhile books include the following:
Gay, G. (2000). *Culturally responsive teaching: Theory, research, and practice.* New York: Teachers College Press.
Nieto, S. (1999). *The light in their eyes: Creating multicultural learning communities.* New York: Teachers College Press.

Solomon, P. (2002). *The assessment bridge: Positive ways to link tests to learning, standards, and curriculum improvement.* Thousand Oaks, CA: Corwin Press.

Thompson, S. J., Quenemoen, S. J., Thurlow, M. L., & Ysseldyke, J. E. (2001). *Alternate assessments for students with disabilities.* Thousand Oaks, CA: Corwin Press.

Teachers Think Systematically About Their Practice and Learn From Experience

One definition of insanity is to do the same thing one has always done but to expect a different outcome. Yet many of us are guilty of doing exactly that. I can't tell you how many times I've been with teachers who've said something like, "I've been doing this same lesson for the past 10 years (or 15, or 20), but these kids just aren't getting it." Well, maybe the problem lies in the lesson, or in its delivery, or in its relevance.

Contrary to popular belief, we don't learn by doing. What is there to learn from holding an open house every year if few parents from your school attend? If we don't learn from holding more open houses, perhaps we can learn by asking ourselves why we want parents to come to school and what they and their children will gain by their being there. Perhaps then we can begin to build an effective program that meets the parents' needs. And perhaps if we put the parents' and children's needs first and then structure our open house—or abandon it and do something else—to meet their needs, we'll enjoy the high attendance we seek. Some schools think systematically and learn from experience. Others, well, they're still holding the traditional open houses that fewer parents attend. The same is true for teachers. For some math teachers, an 80% fail rate means the kids aren't capable. For others it's a signal to try other teaching strategies.

The key to this core proposition is mindfulness. When we become mindful about what we do, when we continually monitor our practice in terms of student outcome, then we can learn from experience. And it's not only teachers who need to be mindful, it's our students as well. In a typical secondary school day, with students and teachers rushing from class to class, subject to subject—begin with a dispatch, end with a closing activity, no time to think critically, only time to do, do, do. We say we want our students to be critical thinkers. Then we have to allow time for thinking, even if that means staring into space in order to gather our thoughts.

Fourth-grade teacher Lynn Gannon Patterson encourages student reflection and provides time for thinking. She reports that, in her classroom, "The most frequently used phrase may be, 'I'm wondering. . . .'" Lynn's fourth graders "know that their opinions and questions are valued, respected, appreciated, and considered to be part of our learning and growing process," which translates into assessment that is "ongoing and internalized" for the teacher and students. Here are 10 consummations of teaching and learning that Lynn created.

10 Powerful Consummations of Teaching and Learning From a Reflective National Board Certified Teacher

Lynn Gannon Patterson

1. Power to strive to meet each and every student's needs—academically, emotionally, socially, and even physically.

2. Power to connect with every student at his or her level and communicate that you care and value each individual's unique individual characteristics.

3. Power to collaborate with colleagues to bring the best program to your class and individual students.

4. Power to make students happy learners who enjoy the process through perhaps a simple play, memorizing with songs, working together in groups, exploring a mathematics problem, reading a story together, researching, sharing, and celebrating our lives through learning.

5. Power to convey to students that the tough stuff is worth the struggle. It isn't always easy but it can actually be a whole lot of fun getting there, and if you work real hard all of that struggle is worth the reward in the end.

6. Power to never stop learning, to know that as a teacher you are a perpetual student constantly setting new goals for yourself.

7. Power to celebrate every opportunity. Sing when you can get away with it. The classroom is your stage, take advantage of it! Celebrate birthdays, teeth falling out, spelling tests, book reports, sharing a book. The classroom is the only place where you are always the star. Go for it! Teachers do in their own classrooms things they would never dream of doing anywhere else. They stand on tables, dance on their desks, wear silly wigs—anything to make a point.

8. Power to never grow old in the classroom; you have to stay fresh and young, continuously learning. It's better than a facelift, a trip to the spa, a massage. It's really okay that we can't afford that stuff, because guess what? We don't need it!

9. Power to make a difference in the lives of children, parents, and the community. Teachers have power. When you say you're a teacher people do perk up. They respect you for doing something they could never think of doing.

10. Power to reflect. Reflection is the most powerful tool a teacher can use.

The greatest impact of the gift of continued reflective practice is providing positive, productive, cheerful, happy student learning. Enjoy your lifelong teaching journey.

I've loved reading and thinking about Lynn's 10 power points, even though I wouldn't celebrate "teeth falling out"—if they were mine.

English teacher Olivia Herring may never have read Lynn Gannon Patterson's 10 powerful consummations, but she follows them in her practice. Like other accomplished teachers, Olivia doesn't rest on her past successes, even when a unit exceeds expectations and even when student learning continues long after the books are closed. Instead, teachers like Olivia relive and rewrite the unit of study, pushing themselves and their students to make the best use of their time. Selecting the material to cover, the essential elements we want our students to learn, may not be part of a universal curriculum, but there is a timelessness and importance when we select resources that lead our students to a deeper understanding of the world they live in and the world they will someday be responsible for. Like Olivia, I learned early that questions, the forming and asking of them, are more powerful than getting the right answers.

Quality Verbal Discourse

Olivia Herring

As soon as I read the first few chapters of *Habibi*, by Naomi Shihab Nye, I knew I had to teach it to my seventh-grade English classes the following year. So many of the main character's reactions to Jerusalem echo my own, and Nye's figurative language captures the mystery and complexity of the city. The unit I developed led some of my students to write an essay on a theme they selected, while others who had mastered such essays wrote on figurative language. More important, the novel and the writing assignments led them to debate questions of morality, cause and effect, values, and responsibility. They owned the themes of fairness, justice, and the individual's place in society. Students grappled with the introduction to a college text on the Arab–Israeli conflict, presented summaries and questions on timely articles and editorials on Israeli–Palestinian violence, compared maps of the region from throughout the 20th century, visited the Los Angeles Museum of Tolerance's exhibit on the Holocaust, and questioned me on photographs from my own study-abroad experience. These supplemental activities enhanced their understanding of the novel as we read about Liyana's adjustments to life in Jerusalem as a Palestinian American. As part of the School for Advanced Studies gifted program at my school, I had the opportunity to create such a unit, reaching to the state standards and beyond to take my students to a place of real learning. The feedback I received from my students still rings in my ears.

As we discuss the month's violent outbursts in the Holy Land, Jonathan, Danny, and others want to know why the Israelis went into Palestinian towns and shot people, destroyed buildings, and so on. They want to know why suicide bombers would give their lives to kill others in Jerusalem. They want to know why they can't work it out, why there is so much violence, what is so special about that particular land. I want to answer. I don't know how. I can give them rote answers about the historical claims people have, answers about power struggles and discrimination. I can explain why the creation of Israel was so important to the Jews in terms of persecution and the Holocaust. They nod sagely at a familiar topic, ahhhh, yes, the Holocaust. They want to know why our money, U.S. tax dollars, goes to fund settlements. They want to know what settlements are and why and how. They want to know if people, regular people like their families in East L.A., know these things. Who's supposed to solve it? What's the answer? Who's right? When will it end? I clear up misinformation, confusion based on them not realizing that Jenin is the name of a town, that Yassir Arafat is a name, and he's a president, well, sort of. It seems every question begs more questions. As much of a cliché as it is, hardly anyone notices when the bell rings. We have more questions, followed by more discussion.

Many of the questions they ask are the real questions, the unanswerable ones, the same ones I asked at the end of my study-abroad experience in Israel, the West Bank, and Jordan. I had more questions than answers, more confusion than when I had arrived. I created the same curiosity for my students, making the unit feel so successful. Although the ethical questions faced by Palestinians and Israelis every day will never appear on the standardized tests faced by my students, the skills and thought processes involved in analyzing such questions are exactly what I would want my own children to practice.

A year later, I wish I had saved more of the students' written reflections to share with my next class. As with any unit, I am constantly adapting it for the next group of students, and the next time around my students will produce some work I can keep with me in a more tangible form. In the meantime, I know that the discussion component of the unit was the most powerful piece. The conversations, questions, comments, and speculations literally spoke volumes. Paul's hand on my shoulder and his question, "Are you okay, Miss?" at the most poignant point of our Museum of Tolerance trip, just after I pulled out my tissue, momentarily erased all the times I reminded him to take out materials, finish an assignment, stay on task. When Jonathan visits me now, he talks about how he and Danny discussed their shock at the corruption and suffering in the world. He says they talk about, "if we had the power, what could we do to make it better." He still tries to fathom what goes through the heads of suicide bombers; he looks forward to my teaching the unit again because it makes some students consider what they would change if they could "go back in time and tell this person to think twice."

Finally, I know why I let myself teach. Why I was willing to step aside from the world of international relations (my major) and Middle East studies (my focus). Why teaching seemed just as important as working with a nongovernmental organization to right the world or go into government to better our international policies. Why the business world seemed so empty to me, the law so distant, and why, when it came down to it, the best way I could do justice to my own education was to pass it on.

Mindfulness: that quality of purposeful living, of paying attention to detail, of continued wakefulness. Mindfulness. Paying attention to our students, to how we interact with them and with one another as professionals and as people. When this story by my friend Janet Hironaka came across the computer screen I wasn't sure what to do with it. Did it belong with a collection of stories about powerful teaching and learning? After all, it's about a stapler. But is it? Janet's stapler is a metaphor for those kernels of beauty and future we can find in every child and in one another. It's about taking risks, sharing ourselves, inviting our students to be part of this whole human experience of which academia and tests are only a piece. It's about mindfulness.

The Prodigal Stapler

Janet Hironaka

The box seemed ordinary for a stapler, so I accepted it from the school supply clerk without much thought, along with the other customary items—a few pens, pencils, erasers, and index cards—and as a teacher new to the school, I accepted my supplies, grateful to receive items for the classroom, recalling that I had often received less at other schools.

I returned to the classroom to set up quickly for the next day. As an experienced teacher used to moving to new schools for opportunities to learn with colleagues and students, I knew that investing time up front to set up the classroom before students arrived would pay dividends during the months ahead. So as teachers were already preparing to leave campus for the day following our seemingly endless series of meetings, I chose to stay a little longer.

As I unpacked my treasure, I realized that the new stapler I had received was truly extraordinary: It was black with a marbleized trim of brown and beige. It was exquisite. I quickly put my name and room number in a conspicuous spot on the stapler for identification purposes. The new stapler must remain in my classroom, but if it wandered away accidentally, someone could help it home. Student learning often requires supporting materials at many points, and I have struggled to provide for student needs to create important products for making critical connections between prior knowledge and new concepts, between new concepts and real-world experiences, I reflected. Thus, the new stapler uplifted my spirit and added dimensional excitement to my meeting my new students the next day.

And as the semester moved forward day by day, week by week, as new faces became familiar names and our classroom discussions developed in scope and intensity, I would catch a glimpse of students using the new stapler to fasten papers to share or to submit as evidence of their work. To them, it was a stapler like any other. But to me, my new stapler was a reminder: I worked in the midst of ordinary paper, pencil, colored marker, glue stick, and the crush of time and urgency of adolescent thought, intention, and production. In this busy, exciting world, I now had something aesthetic and lovely. In the occasional quietness of a class moment, as students were busily recording their thoughts in writing or were bringing closure to their products, a quick glance at the stapler brought me quiet joy.

Often, I tried unsuccessfully to check for the stapler before dismissing class each teaching period, but bells often rang a few seconds before I was ready. It was a task to be sure that the room was rearranged for the next class. Supplies were the least of my concerns anyway. My stapler soon became a permanent fixture on my desk.

And then it happened: My stapler was gone! Its spot was empty. When had I seen it last? What period was it? What had we been doing as a class? I struggled to retrace my steps. The next day, I asked every class about the missing stapler. No one knew about it. And then I did what I had never done with students during my previous years of teaching: I shared my story of what the stapler meant to me in its beauty. I told students about how special the stapler had been, how new teachers frequently had no stapler to begin their semester. At another school, a senior teacher repaired a broken stapler to give me because I had none as a teacher new to the staff, and this took place five weeks into the new school year, after my students had endured five weeks without a stapler and I had had a chance to make friends on the faculty. That school had provided a couple of red pencils, tissues, and index cards. The rest had been up to me.

The beautiful stapler made this school and my work with them very special, I told my students. It broke my heart that the stapler was gone. It was truly the most beautiful stapler I had ever had. And with the telling of that story, I was able to release my sadness. I then brought to school the old repaired stapler I had stored from a previous school. Nondescript, it replaced its predecessor and sufficed for our work in class.

Then one day, Raul, an eighth grader, came up to my desk, stapler in hand. "I found this in a trash can," he said. "It might be the missing one."

Raul had been one of the students I had queried early on when I first missed the stapler. No, he had not seen it. Quiet, with eyes full of thought and perhaps frustration and anger, Raul often embellished his brief sentences on paper with large doodles and dark, fancy, large print. I realized that he knew much and said little. Tall and slim, he looked more like a senior high school student. At times, he frowned, grunted, and acquiesced when I asked for his participation in our classroom activities. At other times, he was moody and distant. Raul rarely smiled.

And now Raul had brought my stapler home. I thanked Raul gratefully and shared my joy. Order had been restored. I set the stapler in its place on my desk, relegating the repaired substitute to a nearby bookshelf. I announced the return to all of my classes and continued our work together.

However, in a quiet moment, I spoke with Susanna, Raul's sister, a seventh grader. I mentioned that Raul had helped me find the missing stapler. Susanna then stated how bad Raul had felt. My joy and sadness, all linked with the stapler, were new to both siblings. Although they could not see the stapler as I did, they had felt my pain at its loss.

I then realized, once again, that my students and I see the world through different lenses, that our point of intersection is in the relationship we share for one period each day within the four walls of our classroom. The beauty of our risk taking, caring, and sharing bonded us daily. As an inexperienced teacher, I would never have shared my sadness and pain with my students. I would have moved on and, perhaps, even have gotten another beautiful replacement for the missing stapler.

Sharing the sadness briefly allowed our joint experience to reach a new level of depth and understanding. I learned from my students that day the stapler came home. My discussion with Susanna gave my prodigal stapler a new coat, an aesthetic patina, and another reason for me to love life in the classroom with students.

Janet was touched by the stapler she lost momentarily, the stapler that stood for beauty and celebration in her classroom. In the story that follows, Susan Sheffield Brandon was touched by a student whose life was lost. I don't mean to equate the two. Of course the life is much more important. What I am connecting here is the state of mindfulness both teachers share. They take the time to be in the moment.

For Susan, reflection also means remembering why you became a teacher, celebrating the successes, not just recalling the times when the lesson falls flat or when the student moves on without achieving all you had hoped for. Susan's story reminds us that we don't always see our successes. Sometimes we know we're successful only through other people's stories. She asks us to keep this story, which is really her story and yours, close at heart.

A Message to Keep Close at Heart

Susan Sheffield Brandon

As teachers, we often reflect upon our experiences in the classroom and ponder the effect we have on the lives of the children we teach. But we are notorious for rarely taking the time to enjoy our successes, for we are compelled to move onward, selflessly. As politics and education become more intertwined it is easy to have days when we sometimes question why we do what we do. When this happens, I think back to the day when I learned a very important lesson: the realization that I do make a difference in the lives of the children I teach.

What could have been an otherwise ordinary day was overshadowed by the impending funeral I would be attending later that afternoon. This was an especially difficult funeral because it wasn't for an elderly person, but for one of my favorite students, Shane, 10, who had been tragically killed in a bicycle accident. I have an extraordinarily difficult time at funerals, so I thought long and hard as to whether I should, or could, attend his. What kind of an example would I set if I sobbed uncontrollably? What would my students and parents think of their emotional teacher?

Nothing can prepare you for seeing children grieving, or for the sight of a child laying at rest. And absolutely nothing can help you hold back tears as you see a mother say goodbye to her child for the last time. Near the end of a beautiful service, Shane's mom came to the podium and with great conviction spoke a few words about her beloved son. She told a few stories about his childhood and I tried hard to focus on her strength and the stories she told.

She told a story that caught me by surprise. She spoke of Shane's school and how much he loved being there. She elaborated about her son being motivated and excited about going to school and how this year he had bonded with his teacher and his new class. She tearfully told how he felt like his teacher knew the "real Shane" and whether he was struggling or succeeding, he knew he belonged. Tears streamed down both our faces. Her eyes locked with mine. A few other students and I squeezed hands. And it was at that moment I realized the impact I have on my students. I had related to Shane on many levels, as a teacher, a mother-figure, a mentor, and a friend.

I know I make a difference in my students' lives, just as they all make a difference in mine.

You see, it's not just the academics we're remembered for, but for the time we take to really understand each child individually. The relationships we establish may seem like second nature to us because we are so committed to what we do, but to a child, it may be the first committed relationship outside of home they enter into. I realized that day that the emotions I was so afraid of showing at Shane's funeral are what define me as the dedicated, loving educator I am today. It's really difficult to brag out loud, but in my heart I know it is important to confirm daily why I love what I do. More important, just as I educate children every day, I also receive through them lessons I need to learn.

Shane, please know I'm thinking of you and thank you for teaching me the most important lesson of my life—to appreciate each day I'm given to make a difference in the life of a child.

Susan goes on to remind us to smile about our successes, not to let ourselves get lost in all the negatives. And, of course, remember to celebrate each child's gifts while he or she is with us.

Marlene Carter is an English teacher in an urban high school. She is also my friend, my mentor, and at times my codirector in the teacher-researcher work we did together. She and her husband are raising three sons. In spite of all the activity in her life, she is restful to be around. She slows me down and reminds me to stop to savor the moment—what's happening, what it means, and why it is important. To remain mindful Marlene finds time to reflect in her personal journal when her students are writing in theirs. It's because she reflects daily that we have this glimpse into her thinking and teaching.

We Are Writing

Marlene Carter

It is the 16th day of the second semester and we are writing.

When this class of 23 juniors became mine in the fifth week of the first semester, they had already bought into a culture of doing as little reading and writing as possible. A change in the master schedule had brought me the class already intact. Their first teacher told me they were a likable group, but that they resisted her efforts to do any challenging work.

At the time, our urban high school was seriously short of books. I went to great lengths to secure literature books that they could take home each day. Unaccustomed to having books to carry home, many of the students complained, "Do we have to carry these around?"

"Of course," I said. "How can you learn about American literature if you only read in this room?"

They carried the books, but resisted the reading. At first they expected me to summarize the reading and tell them what was important. When I wouldn't, they begrudgingly, at first, read along with me and then read on their own in small groups or independently. Over the course of 15 weeks, they became readers who could declare the names of their favorite Harlem Renaissance writers and argue passionately about who was to blame for Gatsby's death. They could compare Native American myths from various tribes and analyze political speeches from the past and present.

Now, during the second semester, my focus was on turning them into writers.

So on Day 16, we again tried to write for 15 minutes without interruption. In my journal I wrote the following:

Most students sit at their tables with their composition books open. Louis is at the one functioning computer. Wilbert is angry because he wanted to be on the computer. Now he sits with his arms folded. Dale has his head down—no—he has picked it up and has resumed writing. Ricardo rubs his head, confused. He checked into class five days late and, despite my attempts to make him feel part of the class, he still appears confused. Aaron, who is also new to my class, is writing. He keeps consulting the sample essay I gave students yesterday.

The girls are all writing. I don't know why they seem to get on task faster. I wonder what they are writing. Since students may use this time to write whatever they want, some students write letters to friends. Others work on writing assignments for this class. Still other students write in journals for their eyes only. I hope that silent sustained writing will give students space to enjoy writing, to write for their own purposes, to get into the habit of writing.

Darien is writing. I am glad. He is a natural leader in this class, and many of the other young men take their cue from him. He has spent time at Camp and evidently is someone who wields some power in the gangs. But he returned to school with a desire to get his education. The first time he spoke in a class discussion, he used vocabulary so advanced that half the students had to ask the other half what he said. In one fell swoop he had elevated the level of our discussions.

Wilbert has stopped pouting. I think ignoring his bad mood worked. He has started writing. Larry approaches me to ask questions about a story he is writing. I answer quickly and get him back to writing, reminding him that he can sign up for a longer conference later.

Four more minutes to go. Carlos has his head down. Dale does too. Monique writes, so does Lloyd who I had to move yesterday because he kept talking out of turn. Wilbert laughs and says under his breath, "This is fun." I wonder what he is writing. Maybe he'll read it to us during author's chair.

In a time when there is great pressure for students to pass high stakes tests, this kind of writing time is viewed by some as wasted time. I know better, though. I know that developing the writing habit takes time, weeks of time, years of time, and that we cannot assume that students will give themselves this time at home. I know that it is easier to teach students to revise and edit if they have a first draft of something they care about, something they are willing to rewrite three or four times. I know that I have students who are overcoming traumatic experiences with writing, who have known only criticism and red marks.

I did not know for sure on Day 16, but I suspected that nearly all of the 23 juniors in my class would come to see themselves as writers by the end of the year. I was right. My students learned to come confidently to the author's chair to read their work and seek feedback. They came to see writing as a process that could lead to wonderful, polished work. They proudly submitted portfolios of their best writing—expository, narrative, and poetry—as evidence of their learning. They became writers.

If teachers are to think systematically about their practice and learn from experience, what happens when a situation arises for which we have no experience? I think those are the moments during which the great teachers show what it means to be an accomplished professional. Immediately following the events of September 11, 2001, students poured into classrooms across the country. What to do? What to say? Do we move on with the pacing plan or stop and examine the events of the day? Marta Findlay-Partridge, a music teacher, helped her students by calling on her greatest resource, the music she and her students shared. Caution: you may need a tissue for this one, I did.

The "Unplanned" Lesson

Marta C. Findlay-Partridge

As teachers, we spend endless hours trying to match our lessons to student needs—sifting through resources, reading the latest research results, consulting professional journals, taking classes in the newest and latest pedagogical techniques, selecting just the right options to facilitate that magic "I got it!" moment. We thrive on the natural high that comes from such planning and successful delivery that leads to student learning.

So, when the events of September 11, 2001, precipitated a sudden deviation from prepared instructional plans, I, like all teachers, found myself in a tangle of colliding emotions. As I sat in my car waiting to meet the high school orchestra students at my third school of the day, I kept asking these questions over and over: "What do my students need now in the face of such horrific images? How can any teacher put these events into any meaningful perspective? What am I supposed to do, just one person among many threading my way through this delicate maze of confusion, pain, and anger?" With a heavy heart, I got out of my car as the bell rang for next period. I had to concede there was no handy multipurpose lesson plan I could reach for—I was going to have to teach by faith and by intuition.

The students stumbled into my classroom, dazed and in shock from the hours they had spent glued to television screens. They met my request to get their instruments with a combination of bewilderment and belligerence. They dutifully set up the room and unpacked instruments, very slowly, almost as if waiting to hear me say, "It's OK—you don't have to play today." But I persevered. These students are normally highly interactive, full of ideas and suggestions. But on this day I had to prod them to select pieces from their repertoire to play, and they begrudgingly complied. I made no attempt to rehearse. For the next 30 minutes, I prayed that the music would speak to their distress as they continued playing the pieces in their portfolios. When I made no further requests, they looked up at me with inquisitiveness. Their intense anxiety appeared to have been replaced by something closer to composure.

In a teaching moment that was both terrifying and touching, I shared this *lesson* with my students:

> When your world is shattered beyond all comprehension and you think you have nothing to hold onto, grab onto those things that are lasting and constant in your life—love, knowledge, and beauty. Because, no matter what, no one can take those things from you, they are yours forever, to use and to cherish as you wish. Take this moment to think about the talent that you have, how you have chosen to develop those gifts, and what you do with them. You go into your community, you bring enjoyment to the elderly and the infirm, you share holiday cheer with people who are lonely, and you enhance the experience of worship for many people. And when you remember all those things, be grateful for the blessing of music in your life and know that it cannot be taken from you—music is lasting, it is permanent, it is solace, it is hope, and it is joy.
>
> Go home and play something you love for your family tonight. As you nurture others with music, perhaps you will be comforted as well. For as you go through life, you will find that your music will strengthen you, that it will speak to you in ways that words cannot, that expressions of horror and sorrow and helplessness and anguish are all there in the music. When things get unbearable, as they are today, where do you think people will turn? They will turn to music. How fortunate you are that you can play an instrument and help in the healing—be immensely grateful. Use your talent for good, use it wisely and often, and carry this in your heart—you are a musician, no matter what happens around you.

Within a week, the students planned their next concert, dedicated to the memory of victims lost on 9/11. They chose some of the most beautiful selections ever written, some even beyond their reach, but they worked hard to learn them; their rehearsal and preparation proved therapeutic. From their sense of purpose came reassurance.

We don't lose ourselves when we become teachers, often we find ourselves. We bring our passions, the things we love, into the classroom. English teachers love to read and it's this passion, the joy they have experienced through reading and writing, that they want to share with their students. It's always surprising, and disappointing, when students don't share the passion. Some of us give up, lose our zest for teaching, and may leave teaching altogether. Others, fortunately, dig in and keep trying. We learn what works through experience and from thinking about our experiences.

What Holly Heard: R. L. Stine in the Classroom

Stacia A. Smith

Reading! I remember vividly when reading *turned me on*. Going into seventh grade, I spent one summer devouring the Nancy Drew series. Lounging in the park or with a flashlight under the covers, it was this series that transformed me into a voracious lifelong reader. Hence, on returning to teaching as a seventh-grade Language Arts teacher in an inner-city urban middle school after a hiatus of many years, I was totally unprepared for students' negativism and lack of enthusiasm for reading. Many students looked upon reading literature as a subject—not as pleasure. Some struggled with reading fluently. Others who could read chose not to read anything. Still others thought it was uncool, feared peer pressure, and had very little home support. Students talked about reading one novel over 12 weeks and expected teacher-generated questions after each chapter. My dilemma was twofold: how to foster a love of reading for nonreaders yet teach the critical literary elements they needed to master to pass our state tests.

My solution was to immerse students in award-winning adolescent novels and teach the literary elements through the authors' eyes. We read, read, read! Dramatic readings were provided by audiotapes for motivation and to model fluency. I became the teaching coach who stopped the tape, then discussed and taught critical literary elements.

"We read that in fourth grade!" some students complained.

"Aha," I said, "but you have not read it through the eyes of a writer!"

I had chosen Gary Paulsen's book *Hatchet* to propel kids into reading. Paulsen delved graphically into adventures that I thought adolescents would find fascinating. He used descriptive language and the novel had sequels for outside reading. Next we read books by Jean Craighead George, S.E. Hinton, and others. Students were more interested than the previous year. However, I still had to cajole many students into reading. There still was little to no enthusiasm for outside reading. I began the next year much like the last, but a chance newscast helped me to link students' interests into a reading program.

R. L. Stine had crafted a teen series (80+ paperback novels) called *Fear Street*. The books were mysteries but many considered them horror stories. The books had teen-oriented descriptions, contained no graphic scenes, had stimulating book covers, and matched adolescents' own thoughts and language. The newscast stated that a school board would decide whether or not to keep Stine's books on library shelves.

Aha! I gathered multiple copies of the series, divided students into groups, and told them that they were school board members. Their task was to read the books and decided whether or not Stine's series should be kept on library shelves. They had to apply the literary elements as criteria. They needed to compare *Fear Street* to the award-winning books we had read previously, such as *Hatchet*.

"The way Stine writes keeps you guessing and in suspense."

"He's [Stine] trying to show us morals. We don't find that in Paulsen."

"We realize that this is not a *teachable* novel, but Stine's very creative and imaginative and original. That's what stories are for! *Hatchet* is not that way. We know he will survive."

"Stine's plots have twists but I would change the ending to this one."

Enthusiasm reigned. Students were excited about reading and talking about prediction, theme, and critical analysis. The class had authentic discussions of books rather than question-driven discussions.

Students requested more of Stine's books to be added to the classroom library so they could borrow them.

Through this experience, I designed a "Gotcha Reading" program that motivated students to read more. In class, we read award-winning literature and I taught literary elements. However, we paralleled the reading with adolescent series or pop culture novels. I filled the classroom library with teen-centered novels. Since series books are predictable, students built their enjoyment of reading yet contrasted how authors used literary elements to create this enjoyment by comparing the series novels to the class novels. Many students generated book reports on these novels based on the use of literary elements. This program helped struggling readers with fluency yet built an enjoyment for outside pleasure reading. By the middle of the year, many students had begun reading beyond pop culture novels and read the sequels of the novels we read in class.

"I can't believe that I have read 37 books this year! I really like this author and plan on reading more of her works over the summer," exclaimed one student. Mission accomplished: a lifelong reader has blossomed.

I don't know what it is that makes some people reflective while others remain in the moment, seldom learning from their experiences, but it is easy to spot those teachers who are reflective. They think about their students, about their teaching, about how to make connections between this lesson and that, between this discipline and another. I just read a science entry for a National Board portfolio by candidate Howard Bauman wherein the teacher began with a study of rocks, because to understand rocks is to begin to understand plate tectonics, and how the earth changes, and then how history has been affected by geography, and why different types of cultures exist in different parts of the world, and on and on and on. I wish that as a student more of my teachers had been as thoughtful about making connections as is Howard Bauman. If they had, maybe I would know more now and have better insight into the interrelatedness of everything.

National Board Certified Teacher Barbara Yvette LeWinter has a view of education that is as all encompassing as is Howard Bauman's view of earth science. Yvette is thoughtful, concerned, and reflective. Where Marlene Carter uses a journal to record thoughts, Yvette reports hers in poetic form, just like Dr. Seuss:

Inspire

Barbara Yvette LeWinter

Children are not products,
Not to be mass merchandise,
Children are our greatest assets,
They are our most precious enterprise.

We can teach till we're blue,
We can pretend that we've done,
More than enough,
For the test that will come.

Don't think so small,
The power we hold,
Is greater by far,
Can't you see what we mold?

The power to start,
The power to stifle,
A glance or a glare,
Is not a small trifle.

The power of our words,
The hello we say together,
Can open a mind,
Or close it forever.

I think of little Aldo,
He stole and he ran,
He couldn't focus or learn,
Till I caught him and then he began.

I remember Dominique,
His self-image shot,
But when he learned chess,
His proud, happy grin, couldn't be bought.

I think of Justin,
An angry, young man,
Who received my letter,
His life just began.

And then there was Adela
Who never spoke or smiled,
Till one day, I inquired,
Then she was inspired.

I think of active Kevin,
Who had a great need,
I had to take time,
Mom, finally agreed.

The power to teach,
Is not in the lesson plan,
When will they learn,
It is in the lady or the man.

The one who's in charge,
The one who is there,
The one who is ready,
To show interest and care.

To be truly prepared,
And to really educate,
We must always remember,
It is our duty to relate.

The atmosphere shows,
The truth is purely seen,
The kids know it by heart,
Their perception is keen.

In this day and age,
It is most clear to all,
That our fate rests most,
With the minds that rise and fall.

So, you can obviously see,
We are mom, therapist, educator, too
We police and we search,
For that most secretive clue.

Don't ever forget
The real true, actual test,
Is not what appears,
But what brings out each child's best.

The potential in each,
Is what should matter,
It's not a silly standard,
Don't let that inner drive shatter.

To teach, it is good,
To motivate, is better,
But our goal, to inspire
Can't be measured by a grade or a letter.

Colleague Janet Hironaka enriches my life, as you've seen from her earlier story in this chapter. Because I choose to consult in our city's most difficult schools, I am sometimes overwhelmed by the task, by the children whose needs are not served, by a city that doesn't seem to care about its urban children. In those times, when a teaching or consulting position in a wealthy district beckons me to come, I call Janet and we talk about why we teach and most especially about why we teach where we do, in the inner city where society says the children don't have a chance. We're there to provide that chance because we know we make a difference. Janet could have retired years ago. On the tough days I ask why she doesn't. And Janet replies:

Our Story

Janet Hironaka

If you ask me why I have continued teaching long into what I had earlier anticipated to be my retirement years, here is my answer:

Kevon seemed unusually quiet that day, saying nothing as his 10th-grade classmates chatted away about a new parent as a stranger. We had been reading and discussing a news article about a pair of babies mistakenly switched shortly after birth. One passed away and one grew into her teens. Now the teenager faced numerous challenges as she was being returned to her real family. Unexpectedly, she was being forced to give up familiar people, familiar circumstances, and familiar surroundings. This was traumatic. And my students imagined how this would be for them and understood this predicament in their own ways.

Toward the end of the class period, after a long period of silence, Kevon finally spoke. In a whisper, he said that this was going to be his story, too. The class listened attentively, and then everyone wanted to know more. In a largely male class, the sprinkling of girls asked questions immediately. How did Kevon get separated from his mother? Where will he meet her? How did he feel? What was he looking forward to?

Kevon would travel to Belize to meet his mother for the first time. He would spend the holidays getting acquainted with her. "I'm scared!" he admitted. He did not know what to expect. He had not known any caregiver besides his aunt. He'd assumed he had no real mother. And suddenly, all of this changed. Now he must meet his mother, a stranger in his life. What an unusual Christmas this would be.

Before we knew it, Kevon left for Christmas break a few days early. Although he was no longer in class, he was very much on our minds. "I wonder what will happen when Kevon first sees his mother?" someone asked. Everyone wondered. I then seized the moment for our writing assignment. Let's all imagine what would happen, I said. Let's all be Kevon and write about what happens in detail. We can all begin at the same place and create our version of his story. Then someone said that we could read our papers to Kevon on his return and then see which story most closely matched what happened to Kevon. And so we agreed.

Together, we decided to begin the story at the airport as he disembarked from the jetliner. We began our drafts in class and continued writing at home. The next day, we shared our papers with partners, provided feedback for each other, and then revised our papers. I visited each student and participated in the process. Editing followed. It thrilled me to see how excited my writers became as they added detail after detail. They were writing with an authentic purpose for a real audience. They visualized events and then searched for words to describe what they saw and how they felt. They wrote with energy and seriousness.

The air of expectancy continued well into the New Year as we returned from our holiday break. But on the first and second days following vacation, Kevon was conspicuously absent. No one expressed it, but I certainly sensed collective disappointment. And on the third day, a beaming Kevon walked in. It had been a truly memorable vacation for him with his new, real mother. And now the students could hardly wait to share their papers. One of the students explained what the class had done. Kevon was encouraged to take a seat at the front of the room to listen as each member of the class read a paper aloud.

With great pride, each student read. Each story was different. Each Kevon was different. Each mother was different. Each story unfolded convincingly as son and mother reached out to each other in different ways. Each story took its place on center stage in our classroom as Kevon listened intently, his chin cradled in his right palm, his right elbow resting on his thigh. His head nodded repeatedly during the readings. He said nothing. He smiled often. After the last paper was read, everyone asked, almost in unison, "So which story really happened?" We waited.

Kevon responded slowly. "Every story has things that really happened to me. You are all right! All of the stories are true."

I had not expected this and watched the class through eyes welling uncontrollably in tears. Members of the class were clearly pleased. They had written their stories from their hearts by making Kevon's dilemma their own. And they had all included truth as they knew it, thereby being correct. What resulted was a magical moment of shared joy.

At age 15, Kevon demonstrated his wisdom and sensitivity. The B-football player who grinned and danced his way to his seat every morning during passing period, the athlete who came to school to play football and basketball, who dribbled invisible balls and caught invisible passes to dodge past real student tackles for his invisible touchdowns, suddenly became the real teacher of our class to acknowledge real effort by real, high achieving honors students.

I knew then, as I know now, that caring and learning have a reciprocal relationship in the classroom, and that living and learning are my way of life as a teacher. Where else but in a classroom is there such joy and satisfaction with real people while earning a living? And why should living and learning end just because a calendar declares that this should be so?

Reading through these stories once again I have a new interpretation of mindfulness. At first I thought it synonymous with reflectiveness, but now I see it differently. To be mindful is to be conscious of the moment, of its importance and implications. To be reflective, however, is to reexamine a time in the past, the distant or the near past. Accomplished teachers are both. They are mindful of every day, of all they do with students and with their colleagues, and in their lives. They are also reflective, going over and reviewing what they've said or done. They examine their students' work in order to gain insight into their own teaching. Although the core propositions are intricately interwoven and none really stands above the rest, it is "thinking systematically" that overlays all of the others. I've been living with these stories for many months now, but each reading teaches me anew about the power of teaching.

REFLECTION

1. What personal and professional resources can I call upon when I'm having a bad day? A great day?

2. When I look at my students' work I see . . . When I look at my students' work I feel . . . When I look at my students' work I wish . . .

3. What do I see, what do I think, how do I feel when I am in my classroom? What do my students see, what do they think,

how do they feel when they are in our classroom? Why is this important to know?

RESOURCES

If you can read only one book, choose the following:

Palmer, P. J. (1997). *The courage to teach: Exploring the inner landscape of a teacher's life.* San Francisco: Jossey-Bass.

Other worthwhile books include the following:

Ayers, W. (Ed.). (1995). *To become a teacher: Making a difference in children's lives.* New York: Teachers College Press.

Darling-Hammond, L. (2001). *The right to learn: A blueprint for creating schools that work.* San Francisco: Jossey-Bass.

Taggart, G. L., & Wilson, A. P. (1998). *Promoting reflective thinking in teachers: 44 action strategies.* Thousand Oaks, CA: Corwin Press.

Teachers Are Members of Learning Communities

There's a good reason why proverbs are handed down from generation to generation and travel from culture to culture—they speak the truth. And so I paraphrase here the African proverb, it does indeed take a village to raise a child.

Teachers tend to go it alone, each in their own classrooms, each trying to solve all the problems kids bring with them and still teach the skills children will need as they move into the community. The reality is that only about 14% of what kids know comes from what they learn at school, and some of that small percentage of learning happens in the corridors, out in the yard, and in front of the gym lockers. Most of student learning happens away from the classroom.

Why do we act like we have to do all of the teaching and do it alone? Let's throw open the doors and bring in other teachers, parents, and community members as partners. Businesspeople and professionals have a wealth of experience that is intriguing and motivating. They're real. Parents are good for a lot more than cutting construction paper and providing birthday cookies. They bring talents and interests and stories of their own. When I did a parent workshop in the inner city, parents learned to use a rubric to score their students' homework. And, they were accurate; they could check their students' homework and did. Your colleagues all have strengths and passions and lesson plans that work.

Core Proposition 5 is about throwing open those doors. It's about working with colleagues, continuing our personal growth in formal and informal ways, and engaging parents and the community as partners working together to educate our children. The most effective classroom strategy I've ever used is student-led conferencing. In these conferences students present their work to their families and talk about their progress. I stand to the side while dozens of conferences go on about me in three or four different languages. The result is that parents learn what their students are doing in school and together they plan how to do it better. The first year I held student-led conferences instead of the traditional teacher-in-charge conferences I was amazed. Students learned more and I did less. What a concept.

Some teachers are breaking through the isolation and engaging parents and community members to become active partners in the education of all of our children. Tammi Bender found a way to make the subjects she was teaching relevant and meaningful while actively engaging her community, the parents, and her students.

A Box Is Not Just a Box

Tammi Bender

Creating a task that truly cultivates a child's ability to achieve is the goal of every educator (or should be). A task should encourage students to consider others' points of view, show true understanding of the ideas given through verbal and written communication, and make connections with the outside world.

In my school district, the fourth-grade course of study includes teaching the branches of local, state, and national government. The fourth-grade curriculum includes various economic ideas such as consumerism, production, and entrepreneurship. Now, all of us know that you could go to the text, *round robin* read the selection, and then assign the accompanying worksheet. We also know that students retain very little of this type of learning in their long-term memory.

Making this a *hands-on* learning experience would make this task more authentic. So based on the hands-on Interact program we created a classroom city. We became Benderville.

To create Benderville, we asked a local construction company to donate refrigerator boxes. One evening, parents and students met in my classroom. Each family took a box and created a business within its four cardboard walls. The parents and students decorated the box and students put their desks inside. We cut holes in the sides so students had a window through which to sell their products. They put mailboxes on the outside. We had a flower shop, a music shop, bakeries, and more. The evening was fun and we became a community of teachers and learners.

Once we had the city, we needed to establish a local government. We elected officials for the judicial, legislative, and executive branches. These government officials ran our weekly city meetings and received payment for their services. We also had a fire chief who fined students whose businesses posed a fire hazard and a police chief who imposed fines for breaking classroom rules.

The students opened their businesses for half an hour each day and sold their products to the consumers (younger students in the building). They put their profits in the bank and the banker calculated their weekly interest earnings. Students were responsible for maintaining their own checkbooks. They paid the utility chairperson the weekly rate for rent, electricity, and trash disposal.

This hands-on approach to learning encouraged students to grapple with such questions as:

If I price my product high, will I make the same amount of profit as my neighbors who are pricing their products lower?

If I make too much of my product and it goes to waste, how will that affect my profits?

What happens if I don't make enough of my product?

This hands-on approach to learning allowed the student to internalize success beyond our school. They experienced local government and entrepreneurship at an early age. Instead of reading about government, they role-played government and they gained deeper awareness about what government means in their lives.

Students were enthusiastic and motivated. They took ownership of their own learning, and I did not do things to or for them, but with them! They made their own decisions and they loved the fact that I was paying attention to what they had to say.

It is this type of task development that gives all students the achievement opportunities that are essential to learning. Appropriate task development forces the teacher to say, *Let's look at us and determine what we can teach better. What do we need to focus on, to learn more about, in order to make learning more meaningful and authentic?*

I came to education after many years in business as an entrepreneur and as a corporate manager. One of the many conditions I found curious during my first teaching assignment was the high school teacher's isolation. Not only was there scant if any time for collaboration and teamwork, but teachers operated independently without any eyes upon them. That couldn't happen in business. There we are always under scrutiny: scrutiny from the clients and from the managers.

So what happens to a teacher who decides to participate in the National Board certification process, which requires an opening of the classroom doors, an exposure if you will, of one's practice? For many this is a daunting challenge, one they are unwilling to take on, perhaps asking themselves, What if my practice won't hold up under careful scrutiny, mine or someone else's? What if I'm not as good a teacher as I think I am? Fortunately many thousands of teachers are opening their doors, more every year, and examining their practice. The result will be a decrease in the isolation that drives many from the profession, higher accountability to our clients—the students and community—and much more powerful teaching and learning.

We've just read how creatively Tammi Bender used construction boxes to help her students found their town. When I first read this story I was very impressed with her creativity and with her application of the essential understandings she wanted for her students. Student audiences are relatively easy to please, especially in the early grades, but would Tammi's practice still look as accomplished when it was examined by her peers? Tammi wondered if she could achieve the high and rigorous standards established by the National Board. Then she gave it a try.

Teachers Are Students Too

Tammi Bender

That's what the truer truth was like, and I was afraid to leave the place where I was...because I was afraid I'd never be able to find it again, never to be able to come back.

—From *The Fall of a Sparrow* by Robert Hellenga
(New York: Scribner, 1998).

I was at a comfortable place in my life. I had been teaching for 7 years and the word on the street was that I was an exceptional teacher. My students were happy, the parents were happy, the administration was happy, and I was happy, but also afraid. So you say why leave this place? Well, the truth is, we all need to keep learning and I was afraid. I was afraid to take risks. Oh, sure I tried new things in my classroom but I never risked having my teaching evaluated and judged by myself, let alone by my fellow colleagues. Why risk it? Things were good and I wasn't one for rocking the boat. My fears were surfacing quickly in my mind. What would my peers think of me if I said something so primitive that it would become the talk of the teacher's lounge? What if my philosophy disagrees with all of the people that I have to work with every day? Would they still respect me when the day was over? What if I didn't know the answers to some of the questions, when I thought I knew them all before?

Now this place that I am talking about is not graduate school. Been there and done that. Yes, it was valuable, but no I didn't take any risks. I followed their prescriptive syllabus like the good little student that I had always been and gave all those necessary explicit answers they needed and walked away with that diploma. No, this place was an after school postgraduate staff development course on evaluating your teaching instruction, tasks given, and assessment pieces. During this class, we took rubrics and used them to assess our teaching strategies, evaluate assessments, and analyze the tasks we gave students. Each rubric was based on a 1–3 scale, with 3 the highest. Using the rubrics forced teachers to rate the authenticity of their classroom practice. It was tough and I was afraid. I mean let's be realistic! How would I handle it if I received a 1 rating on my teaching instruction? That would crush me! Yet I did it and it changed my teaching career. I started rating everything in that classroom and I mean everything! I learned to look at my teaching from a different perspective. I started to say things like, "Why am I teaching something without assessing for understanding first?" "Why didn't that lesson work?" "What made that lesson so successful?" "What am I really trying to teach here?" I began to grow. I was becoming a professional.

This is my story. Invite people into your classroom and share what you are doing. Ask what they think. Question everything you do. Give your instruction an honest rating and continue to improve. Get teachers together and discuss your theories on reading and math. Practice what you preach by continuing to read and to write all the time. Model for your students what you are doing and help them to look at their work more critically. Talk to each other, learn from each other, and do not be afraid.

One of the major impacts National Board certification had upon me was that it encouraged me to be more collaborative and to get out of the isolated classroom paradigm and be part of a community of learners. Teachers are models for our students. We may say we want them to be lifelong learners, but if we don't model our own learning, we'll fall far short. Claudia Swisher not only joined her colleagues during her year of certification, but remained afterward to support the next group, and the next. Along the way she found that she continually learned more than she gave. The same is true in our classrooms. We learn from our students when the community is inclusive, constructivist, and open to the magic of teaching. We learn from our colleagues when the environment is safe, where we can risk sharing the teaching that misses its target and celebrating our successes when they occur.

Sharing What Works and What Doesn't Work

Claudia L. Swisher

Turning into the parking lot on this dreary Saturday morning, I find 23 cars parked neatly side by side. I'm running, as always, a good 5 minutes behind schedule. I rush down the empty halls of the high school prepared to join a classroom of learners. A classroom filled with teachers is very different from my daily interactions with students.

In Oklahoma we tell candidates the National Board process is about telling our stories—the story of our classroom, our students, our growth as a professional. We share the story of our year. We honestly retell the highs and the lows—those awful nights when we lose all confidence and those magic moments that remind us why we feel so passionately about this profession. Candidates ask questions and share responses. Mentors answer when we can. We listen and celebrate, we console and encourage. These meetings have become a highlight of my career. I learn so much from my colleagues. I learn as my friends talk about their classrooms. I learn as I view videos and listen to teachers talk about their classes. I learn as I read entries and look into different classrooms.

We share books. We share professional development experiences. We share our love for teaching. This has been profoundly moving for us all. First-time mentors come unsure what they can offer, whereas long-time mentors come because we know we will learn—a new idea for classroom management, for working with small groups, for organizing a discussion, for searching for meaningful curriculum. We all become more reflective as we hear what works or doesn't work in someone else's classroom and share what does or doesn't work in our own. We push each other to expect more from ourselves and we return to our students with renewed resolve to make a contribution to every young person we teach.

This opportunity to work with mentors and with candidates reminds me why National Board certification means so much—I am a member of an exciting community of learners who value students, learning, and reflection as much as I do. This is a classroom where everyone wins—the candidates, the mentors, and most important the students of Oklahoma. It is also a model for what all classrooms can and should be.

Claudia's story represents an idea: professionals learning from and with other professionals. But her experience is still the exception, not the rule. It's the promise of what can be. Isolation is still a major theme that continues to run through public education. Teachers think they have to solve all students' problems within and beyond the school. And they think they have to do this without assistance from their colleagues, from support staff at their sites, or from the parents and families of their students. We hear too often from too many educators that parents don't care. But that has not been my personal experience or the experience of thousands of educators like you, or like Karen Caruso, whose story follows. When we invite parents to become our partners in educating their children, when we teach them how they can help their children be more successful in school, parents become advocates and our jobs become easier.

The Importance of Partnerships

Karen M. Caruso

When I look back at my first year with Los Angeles Unified School District, I recall not only the students, but also the families I came to know. My class, in Room 17, was a combination second and third grade, which meant a wide range of learning abilities. Many new-to-the-school students were also added to the class. Despite these challenges, I was determined to make the year a special one.

As the year unfolded, I realized that many of the students in my class had emotional problems. Having recently completed my master's in psychology and an internship as a child therapist, I was able to apply my skills with the students at hand. I knew, though, that without families' support I couldn't be as successful as I hoped to be.

I began by setting up ongoing methods of communication with each of the families. There were obstacles: parents that needed to work late hours, split homes, and in some cases severe financial stress. In one situation, the parents had recently separated and Nat's mom, Holly, had relocated to New Mexico. In order to keep her informed and involved, every week I mailed her one of my home/school communication sheets that described what we had learned. I added a brief comment on Nat's progress. Holly often wrote back, and when Nat returned from his once-a-month visit he'd bring an artifact to share with the class. Because of the relationship, Holly knew she could contact me at any time about Nat. In another situation, Anthony's mom was single-handedly supporting her two children while attending school. We scheduled regular weekly morning appointments to talk about Anthony and his successes over the past week or to problem solve, if necessary. Anthony went from low performing to above grade level by the time the year was over. One of my second graders was having so many problems with self-control and violence that his dad left his pager on for me. In addition to these individual meetings, I started Family Evenings. Once a month students and their families came to school for a potluck dinner and an educational activity. These events brought everyone together, thus fostering community among the families. All of these combined experiences made the school year memorable for all of us.

When the first day of a new school year or an open house fills your classroom with not only current students, but also past students and their parents, you understand that as a teacher you have an impact on the people involved in your students' lives. Years later I still recall that special group of parents and students who taught me that a teacher is someone who becomes part of the family when the family becomes part of the school.

Inviting community partners into our classrooms opens the world for students. But sometimes the results are unexpected. Like the time one of the National Board candidates I worked with recounted her experience introducing community helpers to her second-grade class. Her class had met a firefighter, a mail carrier, someone from the local hospital, and a few others, and she finally arranged for a visit from the sheriff. He came into her room, towering over her second graders, and told all about his job. The students were fascinated. They couldn't seem to get enough of him, so when he invited the class to examine the bus he used to transport prisoners the teacher was delighted. This was an unexpected treat for her students. They clambered aboard the empty bus, tugged at the grated window coverings, and then read everything the prisoners had scratched on the seat backs, the walls, even on the windows. That evening when their parents asked what they had learned in school, many repeated the four-letter words "the sheriff taught us." Of course, the lesson in this one is to do your homework and take the time to discuss with the visitor what is and is not appropriate for your students.

Sharon McCubbin, one of our National Board Certified Teachers who holds two certificates, didn't expect any surprises from her classroom visitor. After all, he was a well-known philosopher from a local university and he'd presented to her elementary students before. But what he said to the class certainly took the lid off!

Taking the Lid Off: Social Studies and the Arts

Sharon McCubbin

I teach 6- to 9-year-olds in a Title VII language minority program over a 3-year period. Students remain with the same teacher in a combination-grade class for the entire 3 years. Approximately 60% of the students do not speak English at home, while 40% of the students are highly verbal native English speakers. Our students work at tables or on the floor while engaged in social conversations, thus facilitating everyone's language acquisition and learning. The students are all empowered to be learners and leaders, along with me.

Since my students usually have the opportunity to be with me more than 1 year, and also to know that they have a responsibility to exercise their "voice," they test the waters often in their attempt to see how far they can go on a learning adventure. If the three states of water can be compared to my class, I would say that we are most often at the boiling point, where there is a lot of observable action, movement, and expansion into wide-reaching areas that defy preset limits and lesson plans, thus the expression "take the lid off."

One 3-year cycle of students was especially justice minded, a human virtue that was also well supported by active, outspoken parents. The well-known philosopher father of a second-grade girl came to give his annual presentation to our class. As usual, it was spellbinding. Among the concepts that he effectively presented was the mention of one of his favorite plays, *An Enemy of the People,* by Henrik Ibsen. The students immediately asked if they could put on the play. The very next morning, before I could read the play myself, a precocious second-grade Chinese-speaking student brought the unabridged version of Ibsen's play to read during free-choice, silent-sustained reading.

Well, the lid was off once again! "Forbidden" knowledge called to the students in the form of Ibsen's unabridged play. The students clamored to get a glimpse of the book's message for themselves. I knew this wouldn't be an ordinary day, not that many of them are. Spurred on by the students' request, after a long search we found a version written for middle school students. I enlisted the help of the philosopher's wife to be our play's director.

Auditions were intense, acting parts highly prized, and play practices eagerly attended. Every child had a part in the play and, more important, in the ongoing social discussions about the play's message. Art imitates life, or is it the other way around? The play helped to instill the belief that we have a moral obligation to take a stand for what we believe is right. Unfortunately, the play also taught us that there is a cost for courageous actions, and this message was not lost on my young students. Not one class in our school came to see our play because the teachers considered it inappropriate, just like certain events that took place in Ibsen's play. However, the children's parents attended and at the end stood clapping thunderously and shouting bravos. All the children saw were their parents' proud faces beaming back glorious affirmations of the students' courageous actions.

Mary Hanson, a third-grade teacher, had other lessons in mind when she got involved with the community. She wanted her students to learn about the world, she wanted them to have experiences beyond what she could provide in her classroom. Mary's goal is to open her students' minds so they consider the wide range of possibilities for their futures. She wanted her urban minority children, who come primarily from working-class immigrant families, to know about the free-enterprise system that helped to make America a place where dreams can come true. Mary invited a nonprofit service organization, Junior Achievement (JA), into her classroom and magic happened.

Opening the Door to Possibilities

Mary Hanson

As a third-grade teacher in a metropolitan city in Southern California, I have made efforts to be more than just "the teacher" or "la maestra" to my students—I have tried to be a mentor who provides more than reading, writing, and math lessons. You see, most of my students come from low-income families, where their view of their place in the community has not only been defined by their economic status, but also by the fact that extracurricular activities are limited and their exposure to many things we take for granted (like "take your daughter to work" day) are practically nonexistent. So, whenever possible, I seize any opportunity to bring community members to my classroom to share their experiences with my third graders.

This year, I was fortunate enough to have a Junior Achievement volunteer teach four lessons on business: the business of running a city, a bank, a newspaper, and a restaurant. The students were so engaged by this last unit that we became immersed in the business of being restaurateurs. We investigated weights, measures, and prices as a part of our math lessons. We did a read-aloud about bringing food from farm (supplier) to market (buyer), and, with help from our JA volunteer, designed our own restaurant, from start to finish. The menus the students designed were fantastic! The JA volunteer even went farther than that. Riding on our unbridled enthusiasm, he arranged for us to visit a local Italian restaurant in Old Town. This was going to be the chance for them to see how a real restaurant works!

I must admit I had reservations about this trip. Our volunteer was so confident, and here I was thinking about things like 40 busy little hands near boiling kettles and sharp objects, or worse, someone blurting out some embarrassing remark, but I just put in my paperwork to district transportation and kept my fingers crossed. I gave the students firm reminders to wash their hands and mind their manners. I reminded them that they were representing our school. Most important, I told them not to forget that, until now, all of their trips to restaurants had been as patrons. They were always there to EAT. Now their perspective had to be different: they were there as investigators. Their goal was to come back to the classroom with information.

The day before our trip, I had not yet received confirmation for our bus. A quick call to the transportation office revealed a mix-up in the paperwork. Our transportation director came to the rescue and the next day, we were all piling off the bus in front of Bucca di Beppo! At the restaurant, Mr. Chavez, the sous chef, greeted us at the door. Walking inside the closed restaurant (they are open only for dinner), each child was wide-eyed. The restaurant, famous for its photo-covered walls, was mesmerizing. There were hundreds upon hundreds of pictures, each conveying some aspect of Italian culture: families eating mounds of spaghetti, pictures of the Pope, the statues and fountains of Rome. After the initial shock wore off, the students passed through the kitchens and were seated in the largest seating area in the restaurant. Like magic, they transformed into curious little restaurant specialists.

Adriana, a slight, blonde 8-year-old, indicated the menu on the wall. "How do you decide the prices of the food?" Another hand shot into the air. "How do you know how much to order? I mean, if there's too much left over, it gets spoiled." Mr. Chavez fielded each question without batting an eyelash. Victor was waggling his hand in the air. "What other jobs can you have if you work here? I mean, what if you don't know how to cook that good?" Mr. Chavez explained about his training, and how he had not only learned at a cooking school, but had been trained by the Bucca di Beppo owners. Victor's eyebrows went up. It was like he was weighing the possibilities.

Mr. Chavez got the kids up and around for a tour. After visiting the salad station, the pasta station, and the pastry section (several kids claimed that's where *they* wanted to work) we visited the pantry (BIG cans of tomatoes and BIG cans of mushrooms) where the students saw what buying in bulk really meant. After our tour of the pantry, came the most exciting part, the walk-in freezer. Since each child was invited to step in and experience the freezer first hand, Ivan peeled off his sweatshirt (I hardly ever see him with out it). As he handed me his sweatshirt to hold, I remarked "Need to see exactly HOW cold, huh?" he nodded silently with a Mona Lisa smile. He was usually a boy of few words, but today was different: "What do you do if the temperature goes up or if the electricity goes off?" he asked. Mr. Chavez seemed surprised at this question from such a small boy. "We have been lucky that it has never happened," Mr. Chavez told him. "But if it does, we'd better eat fast." I heard a deep voice laugh behind me. It was our district superintendent, Dr. Percy Clark. He had heard that we were visiting the restaurant and had come down to see what we were up to. Mr. Chavez laughed too. "Hopefully we can get a repairman in here within an hour."

We walked back to our dining area, and Dr. Clark asked the children why they were there. He was as impressed as I was at their intellectual curiosity and professional demeanor. "Usually, this kind of investigation is carried out by our high school students," he said. "You children are starting young."

Our time ran out too soon, and we had to return to the bus. Mr. Chavez was sad to see us go since there were so many more questions. He called to a worker in the kitchen, "Make those pizzas TO GO!" The next thing I knew, we were back on the bus and I was carrying a gift from the restaurant for each child and pizza for 20. Tired, I slumped in the front seat, realizing we had gotten through this with no mishaps, no burned fingers, no embarrassing comments, and I was prouder than I ever thought I could be.

After we wolfed down the pizza and drank half my case of bottled water, we debriefed. We talked about what we'd learned. The third graders talked about figuring out how to make a profit if you prepare a meal. They talked about the COLD freezer and how buying one costs a lot of money. They talked about a lot of things that they saw, including the pictures on the walls. But the part I liked most was that they talked about the possibilities. I can't count how many times I've heard these low-income kids, whose parents are working at low-paying, dead-end jobs, talk about the low-paying, dead-end jobs they will take when they turn 18. At least four kids have continued to talk about going to cooking school, and two more thought it would be cool going around to restaurants and fixing the refrigerators and freezers. Brenda, who had told me more than once that when she grew up she was going to clean houses like her mom, told me that when she was 18, she was going to go to Bucca di Beppo and ask for a job as a pasta chef. "I'd have to start as a helper, I think," she said with serious eyes, "But I could get better!" She smiled and ran out to recess.

Elie Weisel, the author of *Night* and a Holocaust survivor, said that one of the chief purposes of education is to teach compassion. Without compassion we may amass great knowledge, as Brenda Smith reminds us, but then use it simply to kill one another more efficiently. Brenda wanted to teach her students compassion, but that lesson was just beyond her reach until one of her students suggested that they call in the local Marines.

No More Two by Four

Brenda Culp Smith

I was working on my National Board certification and teaching sophomore English, which in our state curriculum is world literature. Students had to pass the state-mandated literary essay in order to receive credit for the course. I, like all the other teachers in my school, was feeling the intense pressure to make my students perform well on this essay test. We were within four walls, two feet on the floor every day, reading world lit and writing furiously. But the writing lacked depth and I lacked the heart for it. I knew within myself that I didn't believe in this "one test on one day in one way" kind of assessment. I knew that there was so much more than this in my calling to become a teacher. The great educational philosopher John Dewey did not believe in two-by-four education, two feet on the floor, within four walls, and neither do I.

At the time we were reading the autobiographical novel, *Night*, by Elie Weisel. The students could not help but be drawn in by its compelling plot; after all they were 15 years old, just like the protagonist. But I heard in their comments a shallowness of understanding, an inability to truly comprehend on any kind of realistic level the setting of the Holocaust that Elie Weisel described firsthand. Their essays were flat and their insights superficial. Two-by-four education could not make the book real for them; we had to go beyond the four walls of the classroom.

At the suggestion of a student, I called on the expertise of our local U.S. Marines recruiter and his colleagues to help us with a role play to simulate the environment of a prisoner of war camp. We didn't wish to trivialize the experience of Holocaust survivors, but instead we wished to give the students just a glimpse of insight into how it feels to be a second-class citizen in this world. It would be their first taste of what it is like for someone else to have complete power over them. And so, the day arrived for what has come to be known as "the Marine role play." One moment we were talking excitedly about how the activity would soon begin; we had spied the Marines arriving on campus. The next moment they had burst into my classroom yelling commands and demanding silence. I could not have predicted how quickly thirty 15- and 16-year-olds, and one much older adult, could line up behind one another, hands holding on to the shoulders of the person in front, stare at the floor, and maintain complete silence: an astounding 1-minute transformation.

From that time on, until 90 minutes later when we returned to the classroom, we all belonged to someone else. We were no longer individuals with our petty differences; we were one group cemented together by a common adversary. We crawled down hills and scrambled up others; we did pushups until our arms could no longer hold us up. We ran, we traded shoes, we carried one another, we measured the length of the football field with our bodies, we did jumping jacks, we carried rocks, we did mountain climbers in the long-jump pit, and we somersaulted across fields. We were yelled at, insulted, made to feel stupid, and felt like quitting. In short, we were treated like second-class citizens in a world run by an elite few with all the power.

A few did quit. A few made it hard on others by not cooperating. But the vast majority of my students hung in there to the very end. And they made it. How did it affect them? Well, when the students wrote about the experience their writing was not flat, nor was it superficial. The experience made a deep impression on every student in the class. A student who had always been quick to judge and make insensitive remarks to others wrote, "I learned that others are just like me and that I should treat them with the same respect I would want....I saw the look in the others' eyes and it made me sad for ever saying something bad to someone....People can become addicted to power."

But the most memorable comment came from a bright but extremely quiet girl who ran up to me when it was over and gushed, "I always wanted to try something like that to see if I could do it! Now I know that I can. That was the greatest thing I ever did in my life!" She selected *Night* as the piece of literature to write about on her state test and wrote one of the most insightful essays I have read as an English teacher.

To be indifferent is to be dead. I think Elie Weisel would be proud of my classes. As a result of a creative learning experience my students are no longer indifferent, but full of compassion, intensity, and empathy.

In too many of our classrooms, we are an audience of one. The teacher reads student work, grades it, returns it, and never sees it again—and most likely neither does anyone else. Consequently, the relationship between the teacher and the student often determines the student's level of accomplishment. I've always been a firm believer of going public, of expanding the audience for student work. Let the work be read by peers, by parents, by other teachers. Send it out to newspapers and student publications. Invite the community in to see what our students are doing. Of course, although I've been published in our city's newspaper and in a few national professional journals, I've never made it to the *Oprah Winfrey Show* as did Audrey Clarkin, one of Michael Taylor's students. Her essay about September 11, 2001, went on the air.

Classroom Assignment:
Get on the Oprah Winfrey Show

Michael Taylor

Too few teachers push students to publish their work beyond the classroom. Fortunately, Pinellas County, Florida, students have several vehicles from which their voices can be heard. Student work can be published in school newsletters or newspapers whose audience may be several hundred to a couple of thousand. *Impressions,* a bimonthly, countywide magazine produced by students for students offers an additional audience of 40,000 to 75,000. The *St. Petersburg Times* newspaper publishes student work on the weekly Xpressions pages and has a readership of half to three quarters of a million.

When students take advantage of these publishing opportunities, exciting things happen. Audrey Clarkin, one of my seventh-grade Language Arts students at Meadowlawn Middle School, responded to a classroom assignment to explore how she felt about the September 11th events. I passed along her essay to the principal, who in turn read it to the whole school via our morning television news program, an audience of 1,300. He read it again on back-to-school night to several hundred parents. Audrey submitted her essay to Xpressions, which published it on September 24th. The next turn of events was most surprising.

A representative of Oprah Winfrey's show called the school. They wanted Audrey to be part of a segment of the December 17th show titled, "Building Strong Family Connections." Apparently, a researcher in search of responses to 9/11 found, via the Internet, the Xpressions site and Audrey's essay. The producer made arrangements to record Audrey reading part of her essay in the form of a letter to Oprah. To accompany the reading, Audrey sent family photos. Audrey got a lot of mileage from her three-paragraph essay. As if the *Oprah Winfrey Show* weren't enough, Audrey and I were asked to tape a segment of *PCS Journal,* a Pinellas County Schools local cable television interview program with moderator Al Ruechel, and give our views on the experience. The show aired on Tuesdays during February 2002 four times a day.

Only 1 of my 145 students was so motivated to both complete and submit the assignment: Audrey. Does her experience guarantee that if every student completes every assignment to the best of his or her ability that student will end up on the *Oprah Winfrey Show?* Of course not. However, if students take advantage of opportunities to go beyond the classroom and get their work published, good things can happen. Another student, who had a descriptive piece about his relationship with his grandmother who had suffered a stroke published in Xpressions, received three letters from complete strangers who were moved by his essay. When students realize they have a powerful public voice and that people will respond to what they have to say, real-world connections to academic classroom assignments occur. As a result, students can find a greater value in simple grammar lessons and essay assignments. When Language Arts teachers and others push students to publish, powerful moments can occur.

Here's Audrey's original essay:

> At first I thought that some building had caught fire. I didn't realize why everyone around me was reacting the way they were. Not once did the thought of "terrorist attack" occur to me. Then, as the second airplane hit the other building, a wave of disbelief overcame me. Even though the sight of the fire, smoke, and ash overwhelmed me, all I could think of were the people who started another normal day of work at the World Trade Center, only to have everything changed in an instant. For the past week the only thing on television has been images and sounds of the destruction in New York, Washington D. C., and Pennsylvania. Pictures have been replayed so many times that I can't close my eyes without seeing them. More heartbreaking than those images are the countless stories and tears of those who are missing their loved ones, or those who already know that their loved ones did not survive this terrible tragedy.
>
> Tonight is different. For whatever reason, my parents don't have the television on in the background. This has given me time to think. Obviously I am not as affected by the events of Sept. 11 as others were, but I have changed. Since that day, I've been thinking a lot about my family and friends. I didn't realize how important they are to me until I saw the suffering of others who no longer have their loved ones in their lives. Many people will say that you don't know what you have until it's gone. But, I realize what I have before it's lost, and I'm determined to cherish those people who are special to me every day.
>
> Before the attack, I worried about getting new shoes, having control over the television remote, and even if we had the right flavor of Pop Tarts (brown sugar-cinnamon) in the house. Compared to children worrying if their parents are alive, parents searching around the clock for their child, and especially husbands and wives cherishing that last phone call from a spouse, my brown sugar-cinnamon Pop Tarts are nothing. I'm not saying that I will never have these little worries again; I hope I do. That would mean that things are getting back to normal, but I think that I won't be as quick to sweat the small stuff. This wasn't just a building that had caught on fire. It was even far more than

a terrorist attack. This unforgettable moment changed the lives of many people, all people, including me.

—Audrey Clarkin, 12 years old

I completed the portfolio for National Board certification in 1999 and missed certification by nine points. I had no interest in redoing any sections the next year and delayed the decision the following year until I missed the deadline, so I only had the final year to try again. I redid the Instructional Analysis: Small Groups entry and the Analysis of Student Writing entry. Part of my inspiration was Audrey's success with her piece, and I used Audrey and her Oprah experience as one of my three students whose work I featured. I was successful with my reentry. Audrey's revisions worked and so did mine.

The older I get the more I know what I don't know. I certainly don't know everything about literature, my major field of study. There's always a book I haven't read, a poem I didn't understand, a grammatical rule I break with regularity. Opening my classroom to colleagues and others enriches my students' learning by providing an opportunity for them to tap into someone else's knowledge. I team taught with a Science teacher, Lisa Jones-Rath, for 4 years and would never teach alone again. Constance Rogers may have been the visiting Art teacher who taught vocabulary, but both she and her colleague were enriched by the experience of teaching together. Team teaching, full- or part-time, is so much easier than trying to know everything and do everything alone. Just as Mikey's brother said to him in the television commercial when he wanted him to taste a new cereal, "Try it, you'll like it."

A Collegial Approach to Teaching Art Critique

Constance M. Rogers

The classroom discussion was charged with excitement. "I think the most important part of the painting is definitely the tornado!" said

Stephanie. "You're wrong," said Tony, "anyone can see the artist wanted the emphasis of the painting to be on the father." "He's right, the figure of the father is the focal point, especially the position in which he's placed, and it creates the balance in the work," added Lannie.

"I think all of you are sort of right, but if you really look at the movement in the composition, it begins in the background," said Josh. "Well, you can't say the main subject of a figurative painting is the depth or perspective, and that's what you're saying, isn't it?" asked Isaac. "Oh, my gosh," exclaimed Katie, "it's all about the father and the tornado. The emphasis is both of them—the power and force they both represent!" "Yeah, look at the colors. They're almost the same shades and intensity of gray, and your eye moves from one to the other if you really think about it," said Walker. "It's like a battle, but you still feel the dad is stronger than the storm. Somehow I feel like everybody is going to make it into the cellar and if anyone is left outside when the tornado reaches them it would be the father and he'd still make it. I just feel it."

The painting, "Tornado Over Kansas " by John Stuart Curry, was my choice for a collaborative project between the fifth-grade teacher and me, the visiting Art teacher, based on the written and oral formal critique of art. In order to critique artwork the students had to learn art vocabulary, the language of art, identifying art elements, and principles of design. Familiarizing students with art vocabulary would, I hoped, help them to move more readily into a discussion and appreciation for art. And you can tell by the discussion recorded here that it did.

Reinforcing student learning through interdisciplinary connections of the verbal and written critique was imperative to the success of this lesson. The collaboration with the students' classroom teacher was a valuable asset. So valuable that it has led to a long-term approach to collaborative teaching with my colleague. We worked closely together so that the connection of the oral and written critique was strengthened. This class was a highly creative group of young students who thrived on intellectual and artistic challenges. The variety provided through our combined teaching styles and the infusion of the evaluation of art into the Language Arts curriculum fed the students' intellectual curiosity.

The continued collaboration with the classroom teacher provided extended opportunities for growth and exploration. My colleague felt the exercise was appropriate for her students in so many ways. First, the assignment provided an authentic audience for expository writing. Students learned that every field has its own vocabulary and to learn it is the entry key. With the proper vocabulary it becomes possible to put one's feelings into words.

"The artist also showed balance in his choice of color," noted one student. "No it's the light—he is showing emotion through the use of lights and darks. The brighter colors that seem to be coming from the storm cellar door, which really should be dark, is the artist saying there is hope for everyone."

It's not easy to come to school knowing every day will be a struggle. Some students, like Lyreesha in the next story, have difficulty gaining access to the curriculum. They don't see college or much else in their future. Yet, Lyreesha and countless other students who face similar daily challenges continue to come. That they come to school at all speaks volumes about their desire to learn, about their hope that something will happen and that some teacher will unlock a heretofore closed door. For many students it's the habits of mind they haven't formed that sets a cycle for failure. As educators, when we step back and focus on more than just the content standards, when we look at the whole child, we see through the outward appearances to the core of the problems that get in the way of learning. We can't dismiss kids by saying he or she can't read, can't write, or doesn't want to learn. We need to discover how to help each child, and we can't do it alone. For schools where every child counts, educators work together to build a foundation for success. Lyreesha was fortunate enough to be in a school with a teacher who cared and a system that didn't want her to be left behind.

Lyreesha

Helene Hirsch

At my middle school many students are falling through the cracks, poorly served by our current educational system. They are having difficulty in several areas, but have no identifiable problem that needs to be addressed through Special Education classes. They're unsuccessful for a variety of reasons: below-grade-level reading ability, lack of motivation, little encouragement to complete homework assignments, and difficulty organizing materials. Together, these created a weak base on which to build academic success. There is potential, but it's hidden. We decided that we had to do something or risk losing these children forever. We created a new class, limited to 20 students recommended by any of a dozen teachers at the site. I volunteered to teach them, anxious to help, and curious about how this would happen. I am not trained as a Special Education teacher, but I've been teaching long enough to let experience, and continuous observation, guide me.

We spent a good deal of time organizing notebooks and backpacks so that homework and class assignments are readily available for the students to turn in. This is especially important to sixth graders as they move from class to class for the first time. The core teachers told me just organizing their notebooks had already had a favorable impact on grades. I work closely with the students' other teachers to support their curriculum and provide the extra attention they need to understand and complete their assignments. On a daily basis, students write down their assignments in each class before the teacher checks for accuracy. When they come to me, we go over the assignment, discuss the material, answer questions, and complete the tasks. Knowing they are going to be held accountable, and having someone there to help them succeed, has made a world of difference. Although the students are relieved to have this additional daily assistance, not every student begins by wanting to be here.

Lyreesha was a very angry student and came to my class under protest. She did not want to be there, but had little choice in the matter. She sat in the back of the room slumped down in her chair and glared at me whenever I spoke to the class. When I approached her, she stiffened and refused to answer any questions. The only thing I did find out was that she did not see the value in doing homework. "It don't matter anyhow." I refused to give up on her, something that had happened all too often before. I was not going to let her slide. She was there to improve her work habits and to raise her grades.

We used our class time for students to do homework from other classes. For many of them, this was the first time someone actually checked to see that they were doing their homework. When they finished, we went over the assignments. We referred back to the instructions and then checked their responses. There was no option to "get lost in the crowd" in our room. I worked with the whole class and got to everyone for several minutes of individual time each day.

It is a difficult process to change a student's outlook from encountering numerous failures to experiencing success. But it works! It's rewarding to speak with Lyreesha's Math teacher and hear him talk about her completed homework and her increased participation. That alone is a huge accomplishment, but she also improved her Math grade from an F to a C. When asked what had changed, she said, "Mrs. Hirsch expects me to get my work done!"

What I learned from this class was how little effort it really takes to turn a child around. We need to see our students, to help them to identify what they need to be successful, to listen to them. And then we need to clearly identify the goals and not let up on them, ever. The key to Lyreesha was to expect her to do well and then be there to enjoy her success.

In my consulting work I assist whole schools as they develop communities of learners. Although I work directly with teachers, I model strategies for students to also become communities of learners. At the beginning of the school year, instead of establishing class rules, my teachers help students to identify the environment they need for learning. When we focus on being a community of learners, we're not competing for the highest grade; we're there to help one another succeed. Students working together in a learning community raise everyone's level of achievement without diminishing anyone.

If I Can Think It, I Can Speak It

Kathy L. Smith

In my 14th year of teaching, a principal asked me to move to a sixth-grade position to teach Math, English, and Reading. I had taught first grade for 13 years, so this assignment was a leap. However, I was confident that I would be successful because I had high teaching standards and they wouldn't change. The assignment got even more complex when I was told I was to be the ESOL (English Speakers of Other Languages) teacher. The students needed to develop skills in arithmetic, reading, writing, listening, and speaking, while acquiring English as a new language.

Class began in September, but one student, a Chinese boy named Peijian, did not enter until February. I felt sorry for Peijian and frustrated for myself. His family had come to town several months earlier to open a restaurant. The children were left in China until the parents could provide for them. When Peijian entered school, he could barely speak English and knew very little written text.

During the weeks that followed, I realized that he excelled in math and was Mr. Personality when he was not in the classroom, but he wouldn't speak in whole-group situations. He did better in coopera-tive-group settings. Little by little, he became more relaxed in the classroom. Students started asking Peijian for help in math and wanted him in their cooperative group since he knew all the answers. The students were very interested in his penmanship, especially his Chinese. Everyone wanted his or her names written in Chinese. We had them up all over the walls. Peijian was easily becoming one of us. Even the students, themselves struggling to learn English, realized Peijian was very weak in Language Arts. He gladly helped them in math, and they offered to help him with reading and writing. Yet, I still could not get him to open up with the whole group until the last month of school.

All the Language Arts students were required to write and present a speech. The school winners would be entered at the county level. This was one of the biggest assignments they had for the year and espe-cially challenging for Peijian. Although he was still struggling with writ-ing and speaking, I wanted him to try. Peijian said, "I cannot. I have nothing to write about." I encouraged him to write about China, about something that he already knew well. He could write however he wanted, but he would still be responsible for presenting his speech to the class.

I will never forget the paper he wrote or his speech. He wrote and spoke in Chinese and in English. The students coached and encour-aged him. We were jointly proud when Peijian finally stood up and gave his speech. It was pretty short and to the point, but he had gotten in front of everyone, stood up, and presented his speech just like everyone else. What a wonderful moment in a teacher's career! The only thing better would have been to videotape it, so he could have seen how great it was. What a confidence builder, for Peijian, for his classmates, and for me, a new ESOL teacher. There is power in community.

Sadly, for the members of this classroom community, Peijian died during the preparation of this book. Kathy Smith offers us the following words of remembrance:

In Memoriam: Peijian, December 11, 1986–May 5, 2003

Kathy L. Smith

Peijian was welcomed with open arms, though barely speaking or understanding English and our American ways. In the 4 years that followed, he excelled in everything he attempted. He was a helpful, confident young adult who achieved outstanding academic excellence, including acceptance into the International Baccalaureate Program. Peijian left our world too early, but he will be remembered for his mark that he left in our lives as we proceed into what our future brings.

So let us remember that our community also includes our students. We can call upon them to help recently arrived students become quickly acclimated to their new school environment. And when a student comes from far away, from Ghana for example, he may need more than the academic assistance Peijian did. He may also need to learn about ketchup.

Hamburger = America

Cecelia D. Lozano

Isaac is a young man from Ghana, West Africa. He came to the United States when he was 17 years old. His father lives here with his wife and young family. Isaac had been living with his grandfather in Ghana, studying English and French. Isaac's father wanted him to learn a trade as well as to learn English and knew that, as a junior, Isaac could attend a vocational school through the partnership between the vocational system and our school district.

Isaac could already speak some English, albeit heavily accented and made worse by a nervous stutter. His trouble came in reading and writing and in understanding algebra. My immediate goal with him, however, was to make him more comfortable with American customs. If students' basic needs of safety and comfort aren't met, then expecting them to learn anything would be extremely difficult.

In Isaac's case, for the first two weeks of school, he did not eat lunch. At lunch time I saw him hanging around the hall outside my room. When I asked what he was doing he always responded, "Nothing. I am waiting," for lunch to be over, I assumed. Finally, I asked why he wasn't eating lunch in the cafeteria. His reply really touched my heart and set me into action mode.

He said, "I don't like. American food not good for me." He didn't go into further detail, but I could see just how difficult a time he was having. I suggested that he bring food from home until he became accustomed to our food. He quickly responded by emphatically shaking his head, "My Daddy don't let me. He say, 'You in America now, you eat American food.'" Hearing this edict, another idea came to me. I took Isaac to the cafeteria and showed him all the choices he had: Taco Bell, Pizza Hut, fruit, salad, plate lunch with French fries. I found some other students from Isaac's class, hoping to get a buddy system going. They eagerly accepted him into their group.

I think that was the turning point for Isaac. I never saw him skulking in the halls during lunch again. When I asked what he was eating now, he replied, "I love pizza and hamburgers!" Isaac was Americanized by way of his ESL (English as a Second Language) compatriots from Mexico and Central America.

Isaac's reading and writing improved, and it was to his credit that it did so. Although he could speak three languages, he wasn't literate, having only begun to study reading and writing as an adolescent in Ghana. During ESL class, I adapted content for Isaac so he could understand and pass his core classes. During another class period, I worked with Isaac individually to improve his reading and writing, as well as to help him understand algebra, which was difficult at best since he didn't know his times tables by heart. Confounding Isaac's speaking ability was his speech impediment. I referred him to our school speech pathologist who worked with Isaac twice a week. Working as a team showed Isaac we cared and is what helped him overcome his anxieties in entering a new country, culture, school, and family. He really tried and he was always upbeat and smiling, wanting to learn more and more.

A year after Isaac graduated from high school, he paid a surprise visit. He said he had brought me a gift. He was humble, but proud. I opened the package and found a beautiful, authentic, traditional Ghanan dress. He explained that his father had recently returned from a trip to Ghana and had asked Isaac what gifts he wanted to bring back for him. Isaac told him he wanted something special for his favorite teacher. I was moved to tears as I saw this proud young man honoring me with his heartfelt gift.

Every child deserves to have a highly qualified teacher, not just once in a while, not just by chance, but every year in every subject. Our national whine is that there aren't enough teachers, but we have it all wrong. There are plenty of teachers. More teachers enter the profession every year than are needed. We don't have enough teachers because they leave in greater numbers than they enter. Novice teachers who have the benefit of an on-site mentor during their first years have a 70% higher retention rate than those who don't. If we care about kids, if we believe that a sound education is the foundation for democracy, then we have to open our classroom doors. We need to create collegial environments where we mentor our novice teachers, where we share ideas and lessons, successes and failures with colleagues. Schools can be extended families where everyone cares about all children, where local businesses become teaching partners that welcome students into their establishments. This vision is not just whistling in the wind. Read the stories above. Every teacher went beyond his or her own walls.

Core Proposition 5 is also about advocacy. We can't continue to be lone voices, complaining in the faculty cafeteria and then returning quietly to our classrooms and the students we love. Practitioners have to be constantly vigilant. We have to guard students against policies that harm them. We may not have become teachers expecting to defend public education, but that role comes with the territory. If we don't speak out for what is best for students, who will?

REFLECTION

1. How might students benefit by having parents examine their schoolwork?

2. What are the benefits and risks involved in having administrators, colleagues, parents, and community members examine my students' work?

3. What scares me about opening my classroom for others to observe? What excites me?

4. How can I invite others to partner with me in teaching the students?

RESOURCES

If you have time for only one book, choose the following:
Education Commission of the States. (2002). *Learning that lasts: How service-learning can become an integral part of schools, states, and communities*. Denver: Author. For more information about service learning and school communities, see www.learningindeed.org and www.servicelearning.org.

Also worthwhile are the following:
Benson, B., & Barnett, S. (1999). *Student-led conferencing using showcase portfolios*. Thousand Oaks, CA: Corwin Press.
Comer, J. P., Ben-Avie, M., Haynes, N. M., & Joyner, E. T. (1999). *Child by child: The Comer process for change in education*. New York: Teachers College Press.

Elias, M., Arnold, H., & Hussey, C. S. (Eds.). (2003). *EQ + IQ = Best leadership practices for caring and successful schools.* Thousand Oaks, CA: Corwin Press.

Katzenmeyer, M., & Moller, G. (2001). *Awakening the sleeping giant: Helping teachers develop as leaders* (2nd ed.). Thousand Oaks, CA: Corwin Press.

National Commission on Service-Learning. (2002). *Learning in deed: The power of service-learning for American schools.* Battle Creek, MI: W. K. Kellogg Foundation.

Conclusion

Those Who Can Teach, Do

When I first changed careers, leaving a well-paid job in a high-rise tower that overlooked the city, my coworkers thought I had lost my mind. Why would someone take a 50% pay cut to work in the inner city with students whom they believed didn't even want an education?

I've never looked back. I am where I need to be, doing the work I'm supposed to do. I could give you all sorts of reasons why I teach, as could each of the teachers whose stories are in this collection. Although there's a disparaging saying that goes around in some circles—*Those who can, do; those who can't, teach*—I totally disagree. More accurate is the following: *Those who can teach, do.* Special Education teacher Rebecca Witt provides one of the finest examples, one of many, why so many of us love teaching and love our students. Our rewards don't always come in the form of a paycheck (although they should), but they do come in the impact we make on people's lives. Be prepared to shed a tear as you read about David and his gift of a rose.

David's Rose

Rebecca Witt

I will never forget David, a student in my class during my first year after moving to the district in which I now teach. That year I taught in an alternative education classroom, responsible for 22 at-risk students in

175

Grades 6 through 8. Many had already been retained one or more times in their short academic careers. Most came from home situations that presented them with a great many challenges on a day-to-day basis even before they came through the door of the schoolroom. Few had even the smallest remnant of interest in what school had to offer them, and all felt that their teachers and the school system in general had pretty much let them down for as far back as they could remember. And for many of them, we had.

When I met David he was a 15-year-old eighth grader, raised alone by his father ever since his mother left. He and his father lived in a house trailer with no electricity in a backwoods area quite a distance from our school. He wore the same clothes to school every day—the shorts and T-shirt that he had been given for PE. From the first day I met him, I was ardently aware of the fear and distrust that lay just under the surface of this child's countenance. One look in his eyes told a more incriminating story than any words could ever articulate. David had decided that articulation was of little use to him in confronting daily obstacles; somewhere along the way he had simply decided to discontinue any form of verbal communication, at least with any adult who represented authority or who may expect anything from him. He didn't do written work and he did not participate or show interest in any of the class activities.

At first I had no inkling as to how to approach the task of educating this child. I decided to proceed with David in as normal a mode as possible. I sat beside him, offering instruction and conversation as though I was receiving the desired responses. I would pick up his pencil and write his work as I spoke, encouraging him the whole time about his progress and ability to improve his skills. For several months this continued, with no change for the better or worse in David's effort, attitude, or demeanor.

One morning everything changed. Another student approached me with David in tow. He informed me that David wanted to ask me a question. Day by day, more questions followed, with David scheduling a daily appointment. He often wanted to seek advice about issues he faced as he struggled to maintain his daily equilibrium. I answered his questions honestly, never minimizing his plight, but always trying to teach strategies for coping with his situation. Mostly, I offered encouragement and the promise of a time in his life when he would not find himself entirely outside the realm of control of the circumstances of his life. He responded by putting forth an effort to receive academic instruction and to improve his skills.

About a month before the end of the school year, David announced he was leaving to go live with his mother. On David's last day, I was surprised by a rose in a vase he placed on my desk. David had scrounged up a little money somewhere and walked the 12 miles from his home to school that morning in order to stop at a store and purchase the good-bye gift. He presented it to me in front of the class and left to fill out his withdrawal forms in the office. Later in the day, as I was cleaning out his desk, I found a note he had written that he'd addressed to the class. It offered the following advice: "Mrs. Witt has helped me. If you listen to her, she can help you, too."

Nineteen years ago, David walked out of my classroom, but the impact he had on me that morning has never left my life. He taught me to never judge a student at a glance, but to always seek what lies beneath. He taught me that students, like all humans, will respond when shown honesty, respect, and caring. Probably the greatest lesson David left me with was a profound understanding that we as educators can never really know the effect we have on our students and that it is our serious responsibility to be ever vigilant in maintaining the highest ethical, moral, and professional standards in the roles with which we have been entrusted.

The stories you have read are all true. We've collected them from teachers throughout the country. We recorded them here as they were told to us, with minimal editing. They're stories about the children we teach, about their learning and ours. They are about our good days and bad, and about returning to something we love. The voices you hear in these pages are those of teachers "who refuse to harden their hearts, because they love learners, learning, and the teaching life" (Palmer, 1997). These stories speak to the relationship between one's inner life of mind and spirit, and teaching. That these stories come from around the nation, from different school settings, matters little. Although the stories come from a widely diverse group of teachers they demonstrate that we are all doing the same work, that of service. You come away thinking of students who have entered your classrooms and of others who have left. You think of your own life as a student and of the teachers who have touched you. Stories will spring forth from you.

Stories have the ability to inspire, to teach powerful lessons, to illustrate the possible, and to help us envision what can happen in our own lives and in the lives of students. These stories are also dynamic advocates for public education. They represent what is happening in tens of thousands of classrooms. They hold within them the power of what could be if all teachers and schools provided opportunities for all children to experience powerful teaching and learning. School reform will never happen through restructuring alone, nor will rewriting curricula, revising texts, or mandating more tests improve education. For every child to have equal access to accomplished teaching we need to nurture the classroom, the students, and the teachers. It is the human heart that is the source of good teaching.

But now, for just a moment, let's leave truth behind and imagine a time and place where accomplished teachers are valued as much as movie stars and baseball pitchers, a time when teachers have agents.

Show Me the Money

Marlene Carter

At 7:00 A.M. Rob Carpenter was ready to make his first call of the day. He hoped to close 10 deals by 3:00. Shuffling through a stack of files, he decided to start with Karen Wrobleski's. With one call to Albert Peterson he could iron out the last details. He dialed Peterson's direct line, bypassing the administrative assistant.

"Hello." The voice on the other end sounded annoyed.

"Rob Carpenter here, Mr. Peterson. Sorry to call you so early, but I wanted to wrap things up so I can get the contract signed by close of business today."

"Oh, yes, Carpenter." The voice perked up. "I'm sure we can reach some sort of agreement today. Have you discussed my offer with Ms. Wrobleski?"

"Yes."

"And she's accepted?"

"Well, not quite. There are a few details that we still need to work out."

"Such as?" Rob detected some anxiety in the voice.

"Such as the number of classes Ms. Wrobleski will be teaching. You have her in the schedule for four classes. She'll only be able to teach three."

"I need her all four periods."

"But the District Office has already signed her for 40%. She's only got 60% left. Sixty percent of 5 is 3. You do the math. We have."

There was an obstinate silence. Rob wondered if he had gone too far, but he had to push. "This is a deal breaker, Mr. Peterson. She's got two other offers...."

"Okay," the voice snapped. "Three classes. And she'll still write that grant we need?"

"Of course. At $75 an hour. How many hours do you think this grant writing will take?"

"Seventy-five dollars an hour! We don't have that kind of money."

"Check your budgets. I'm sure you can find the money. After all, if you get the grant—and Karen's about 90% sure that you will—your budget will increase by $100,000. It's worth paying a little up front. Maybe you can use some of the money the school board was going to use to remodel their private bathrooms. Now that the public knows, you're not going to be able to spend it on new tile."

Peterson sighed. "I'll see what I can do."

"All right. We'll make the grant writing contingent upon your finding funding for the planning time." Rob paused to make a notation in Wrobleski's file. "Now, about her room...."

"We gave her her own room." The voice sounded eager to please. "She won't have to travel to three different classrooms."

"Of course. We can't expect Ms. Wrobleski to do her best work if she's worn out. I am concerned, though, that the computers aren't functioning, there are no white boards, and, frankly, the room is filthy."

"How did you..."

"How did I know? I sent a man by to check the location. Our agreement requires 'an exemplary context for teaching and learning.' We take that to include room environment. She's allergic to chalk. She needs the computers for writer's workshop, and dirty floors interfere with her creativity."

"I've put in a work order. I think we can have things fixed up soon."

"Well, she won't be able to report until you do."

"I don't believe this!" the voice yelled.

Rob had to move the phone away from his ear. He pushed his chair back and stood as he replied, "If you can believe that you're getting a National Board Certified Teacher with 34 years of teaching experience, who is also a codirector of the Writing Project, skilled in teaching programs for at-risk students and International Baccalaureate scholars, who writes grants and conducts professional development series for the second largest school district in the state. If you can believe that she is willing to teach at your school when most other people are afraid to come by and visit. If you can believe that, then believe that you will meet every condition or Ms. Wrobleski will be teaching somewhere else!"

The voice was humble, accommodating. "All right, Mr. Carpenter. I'll take care of everything. Just get her to sign."

"Okay. Now, about salary...."

REFERENCE

Palmer, P. J. (1997). *The courage to teach: Exploring the inner landscape of a teacher's life.* San Francisco: Jossey-Bass.

Index

**CORWIN
PRESS**

The Corwin Press logo—a raven striding across an open book—
represents the union of courage and learning. Corwin Press is
committed to improving education for all learners by publishing
books and other professional development resources for those
serving the field of K–12 education. By providing practical, hands-on
materials, Corwin Press continues to carry out the promise of its
motto: **"Helping Educators Do Their Work Better."**